SO YOU'RE GOING TO WEAR THE KILT

SO YOU'RE GOING TO WEAR THE KILT

J. Charles Thompson, F.S.T.S.

with a Foreword by Andrew MacThomas
of Finegand

Illustrated by Bill Thomson
and the author

LANG SYNE PUBLISHERS LTD.

First edition 1979
Scottish edition, Edinburgh 1981
Second enlarged edition 1982
Third revised edition 1989

By the same author
co-authored with D. C. Stewart
SCOTLAND'S FORGED TARTANS

Published by Lang Syne Publishers Ltd.,
45 Finnieston Street, Glasgow G3 8JU
Tel: 0141 - 204 3104

Printed by Dave Barr Print,
107 Coltness Lane,
Queenslie Industrial Estate,
Glasgow G33 4DR
Tel: 0141 - 766 3355

Reprinted 1994, 1995,1997 and Printed 1998

ISBN No. 185217 126

Front cover: Replica of Tartan Room, Balmoral, as featured at the
Scottish Tartans Museum, Comrie, Perthshire

CONTENTS

APPENDIX

FOREWORD

This readable and handy booklet on Scottish attire provides a compact guide not only for those starting to wear Scottish dress, but also for those who may have been wearing the kilt for some time.

The author has provided an authoritative guide for all Americans—and indeed for many Scots in Scotland. This booklet contains much valuable information and useful comment, and I can recommend it to anyone possessing or considering the acquisition of the kilt.

Indeed, there is so much tradition and controversy associated with Highland dress that it is no wonder that many people are confused and anxious to seek advice on the subject. Everything you will be required to know will be found in the following pages.

The kilt is the finest national dress in the world and should be preserved as such. It should be worn correctly. If you follow the information provided in this guide, you will not go wrong.

Andrew MacThomas of Finegand
19th Hereditary Chief of Clan MacThomas

Edinburgh
October 1978

PREFACE

I do not claim to be an expert on Scottish attire in my own right. However I have worn the kilt about as much as anyone else I know in the United States and I have read everything I can find on the subject. I have also made a serious study of tartans and can claim to know a reasonable amount about that subject. Consequently after I wrote a series of articles on the tartan for the *Highlander* magazine, I was asked to do a couple of articles on Scottish attire. These were well received past all expectation or deserving, and people started writing and even phoning me long distance with questions about Scottish attire.

The end result has been this booklet. It is a mixture of data cribbed from other sources, facts that are, or should be, common knowledge, and my own personal opinions. I have made no real attempt to be objective, but I have tried rigorously to label my own opinions as such wherever I have let them into the final text. I have said in the text, and I say again: do not take any of my opinions as authoritative, but feel free to disagree with any or all of them! If, however, you are just starting to wear the kilt, it is much better to be guided by common practice, the experience of those who have worn the kilt for a reasonable time, or even the opinion of purists. I am not a purist in matters of Scottish dress, but I have been careful to include the opinion of those who tend to that extreme. Again I have tried to label it as the purist viewpoint, if only to preserve a balanced view of the subject.

As the title indicates, this booklet is directed to the beginner in Scottish attire. At the same time, it strives to be a fairly complete discussion of the subject. If some parts of it seem to tell you more than you need to know at the very beginning, just concentrate on what you do want to know now. The rest may prove useful to you later.

I am indebted to a great many people for help and advice in the preparation of this book, so many that I could hardly list them all. However I must mention Capt. T. Stuart Davidson, F.S.A.Scot., founder and Vice President of the Scottish Tartans Society, who read the whole first draft of the manuscript and made numerous, most valuable corrections and suggestions.

THE THIRD EDITION

We have another edition instead of just another printing, since there are a minor correction or two, a few substitutions and additions, and a minor change or two in the illustrations.

We have gone more fully into the subject of wearing campaign ribbons, giving the rules of the Scottish-American Military Society.

We have expanded the section on "Accessories" and changed the name to "Weapons," since that is what it is all about now.

And we have added a note, quoting the remarks of Sir Crispin Agnew, Rothesay Herald, in *The Highlander* on the use of the clan crest badge on notepaper.

It remains to thank the loyal supporters of the earlier editions and the readers who look into this one.

If you would like to discuss anything in the book, drop me a line in care of the publisher, or call me at (703) 241-7077. If I'm not home, though, you'll get a recording, but if you can't get me at all, it will likely mean I have taken my final departure for *Tir nan Og*.

SO YOU'RE GOING TO
WEAR THE KILT

Congratulations!

The first consideration is a state of mind—your state of mind the first time you wear a kilt. I don't mean to a meeting of your St. Andrew's Society or some other occasion where everyone is in the kilt; I mean the first time you wear it downtown by yourself in daylight. You will be as nervous as a cat in a meeting of the American Kennel Club. There is no reason to be, for with experience you will find that everyone likes to see a man in a kilt. But every time you hear someone laugh, or whistle, or honk his horn, or say, "Hey!", you will be sure it is meant for you. Of course, it isn't. Next time you are on the street—in trousers, I mean—make a point of noticing how many laughs, whistles, horns, and shouts you hear every day and ignore completely! Then when you blossom forth in your kilt, ignore them just as completely! They will not have anything to do with you except in your heated imagination.

People will look at you in a kilt; in fact almost everyone you see will say hello. If you want to get used to this (to a somewhat lesser degree) start by wearing a Balmoral bonnet with badge instead of your usual hat! You will be amazed at the number of strangers who will smile and greet you as you pass. This has to do with a fact of our culture known as "eye contact." It is rude to make eye contact with a stranger. If you happen to be looking at a stranger when he looks up at you, you must look aside immediately—"break eye contact." There are only two alternatives: to stare at him rudely, or not to treat him as a stranger, that is to smile and greet him. When you are

1

wearing a bonnet, even more so a kilt and bonnet, strangers may look at you pretty fixedly. When you catch their eye, they are not prepared to look away immediately, so they say hello to keep from appearing rude. So in a kilt, all the world is your friend.

Remember that in the kilt you are not wearing a costume. Where other forms of national dress are called costumes, ours is always Scottish "attire." The late Duke of Windsor did not enhance his image with the Scots when he wore Highland evening dress to a costume ball. Just as Scottish attire is not a costume, Scottish costumes are not generally appropriate at Scottish games or other gatherings. Some of the older styles such as the *breacan feile* and *peitean* (both discussed later) are being revived, and one sees shirts in the colonial style worn with the kilt. Purists object to all three of these, though I do not necessarily agree, but what I am talking about is an outfit reminiscent of a MacIan print, complete with targe and an assortment of weapons. To me these look ludicrous, and the implication that I, too, am in costume because I am wearing the kilt shows a complete lack of understanding of Scottish attire. The kilt is perfectly normal dress for a man of Scottish ancestry or connections, and anyone who feels differently is simply displaying his ignorance. At a Saint Andrew's lunch, one member said he could not wear his kilt to the office, because of the way the fellows would make fun of him. Another man rejoined, "Nobody ever made fun of me wearing a kilt. A lot of people have tried, but no one ever succeeded." That is the spirit to develop.

This is the reason for the old saying, "If you can imagine any circumstances under which you would be embarrassed to wear the kilt, then you should not wear the kilt under any circumstances." This is not to advise against wearing the kilt. It just means you should develop the attitude where you would never feel embarrassed to wear it.

THE BONNET

You may want to wear your bonnet while your kilt is on order, to get used to the eye-contact thing, so we will discuss bonnets first. There are two types, the Balmoral, which comes in several styles, and the Glengarry, which is more like a military overseas cap. The latter is a military style, and to many people it looks out of place except with a uniform or on a boy who is young enough not to look silly "playing soldier." One of the books says that certain of the clans prefer the Glengarry, but some of my Scottish advisors ridicule this and have no use for a Glengarry for anyone of any age who is not forced to wear it by military regulations. On the other hand many Americans do wear the Glengarry bonnet—enough so that it would take a bold and dedicated purist to call them wrong. The Glengarry comes in Navy blue with a red toorie (the little pompom on top) and may be "diced" with a checkered band of red, black, and white around it (see fig. 1a).

They also make Glengarries in tartan, but no tartan bonnet is correct with Scottish attire. The same is true of the tam-o'-shanter, a large bonnet in soft wool in tartan colors. Since it is crocheted or knit rather than woven, the tartan design cannot be reproduced. These colored bonnets may be all right to wear with Saxon* clothes to indicate your Scottish predelictions, but do not wear either of them with the kilt!

----

*Throughout this piece, "Saxon" is used to mean "non-Scottish." To some Scots "bloodySaxon" is one word, as "damYankee" is to some Americans.

3

4

Figure 1. Bonnets. a) The Glengarry is worn tilted well over to the right. b) the Balmoral is worn straight and well forward on the forehead. The top of the bonnet is pulled over to the right side. With both bonnets the ribbons are in the center of the back.

The Balmoral comes in Navy blue and several other colors, including tan and blue-green. They are available with or without dicing. The dicing on the dark one is as in the Glengarry, but the other colors have the diced band in the color of the bonnet combined with either white or a darker color. Dicing is said to be the remains of the ribbon that adjusted the size of the bonnet. It is definitely a military style, particularly on the dark bonnets. I personally prefer an undiced bonnet, but both are equally correct. For evening wear, the bonnet should be dark, so your choice for your first bonnet should be a Navy blue Balmoral. This is perfectly proper for day wear, too.

The edge of the bonnet is bound with grosgrain ribbon, and there are two matching ribbons hanging down from the back. There is also a cockade of the same ribbon over the left temple. The ribbons and cockade afford several possibilities of going wrong in wearing the bonnet. First the ribbons: on the Glengarry bonnet the ribbons are always left hanging loose. With the Balmoral there is some disagreement. Some of the experts insist that the ribbons of the Balmoral should always be tied in a neat, small bow. How to do this is described in the appendix, p.102.Nobody says it is wrong to knot the ribbons; some just feel that you don't need to. You will be safer to knot the ribbons. Most people do, and nobody objects to it. I have even heard the romantic notion that knotted ribbons mean that the wearer's affections are engaged, while free-flowing ribbons mean that his fancy is equally free. So if your wife or girl friend reads this, she will probably insist on a knot in the ribbons right now. One man I know just said, "the Heck with it!" and cut the ribbons off his Balmoral. Probably no one has ever noticed.

The ribbons of either bonnet, whether tied or loose, should always come in the middle of the back of the head. This brings the cockade over the left temple, where it belongs. The illustrations show the angle to wear the bonnet. The Balmorals are worn pretty straight, but the top of the bonnet pulls over to the right. The Glengarry is cocked over well to the right. American uniform regulations for the overseas cap, two fingers above the right eyebrow, two fingers above the right ear, are just about right for the Glengarry, too.

Finally, I don't like a bonnet with a bare cockade. The clan badge—your chief's crest surrounded by his motto on a buckle and strap—is the commonest choice. The buckle and strap are the sign that the crest is not your own. It is not correct to wear another man's crest without this acknowledgement that you make no claim to owning it. The history of this tradition is outlined in the next section. If you have your own personal coat of arms, you can use your own crest and motto. In this case, the motto should NOT be on a buckle and strap, since you do own the crest. The motto should be on a plain circlet or some other form of scroll. If you want to go so far as to have your wife and children wear your crest, rather than a clan badge, they should wear it with a buckle and strap, showing them as your heraldic dependents. It is usual, however, for a person to wear his own crest (on a plain circlet) or that of the chief of his family or clan on a buckle and strap. The chief, and he alone, will wear that crest on a plain circlet, since he is the owner.

If you have neither arms of your own nor a clan connection, you may still wish to wear something pinned to the cockade. When I first wore a bonnet, I was told—I can't remember by whom—that this was not optional, and I wrote it so in the first edition of this book. I have been set straight on this by several Scots who know far more than I do about the subject, so I must concede that a bare cockade is perfectly correct. Perhaps because of my early indoctrination, however, it still doesn't look right to me.

Once you have the badge on the cockade, you had better bash the catch with a rock or something, so that the badge cannot be removed. Unfortunately if you leave your bonnet in checkrooms, it is all too likely that sooner or later it will come back to you with the badge missing. Of course you never have to leave your bonnet in a checkroom, and that is perhaps the better course. If your kilt jacket has shoulder straps, you can tuck the bonnet under one of them while you are not wearing it. If you are wearing a jacket without straps, you can tuck the bonnet under your sporran strap or chain. The badge will keep it from slipping out as long as you are not dancing or similarly active. These dodges only work of course when you are in Scottish attire. If you wear your bonnet with Saxon clothes, as we have recommended, the only expedient is to de-activate the catch on the badge.

The cockade should be arranged so that a sprig of a plant may be tucked in behind it. This is not done as commonly as it might be, but each clan has its own plant badge. Some of them, like whortleberry and bog myrtle, are not found in the United States, but the closely related cranberry and ground myrtle (periwinkle) are acceptable substitutes.

In Scotland a chief may wear three eagle feathers in his bonnet, a chieftain two and any gentleman with his own arms one. This does NOT apply to "chiefs" and "chieftains" of American clan societies. If such a person wore a feather in his bonnet in Scotland, he would be an object of ridicule to all who saw it. Unless the Lord Lyon, who controls all Scottish heraldry, has recognized the right in each individual case, it is in the worst possible taste for an American to wear a feather in his bonnet. This does not apply to the piper's blackcock tail. We are speaking only of the one, two, or three eagle feathers that mark the armiger, chieftain, and chief. Nothing about bandsmen's outfits should be used as a guide for the normal wearing of the kilt. Bandsmen are in uniform, which features many things that are entirely unsuited to daily wear. These include spats and the hair sporran and the daytime wear of diced hose and a dirk. We will see later that none of these is recommended.

Two things you may want to change on your Balmoral, the toorie and the cockade. The toorie on the dark Balmoral is commonly red, but many people prefer a matching toorie, as on the Balmorals of other colors. The cockade is black on the dark Balmoral, because the British military cockade has been black since Hanoverian times at least. If you object to the Hanoverian color, you may prefer the white cockade of the Jacobites or a blue cockade for Scotland. Another choice is the livery colors of the arms whose crest appears in the badge. You may have a bit of difficulty determining those colors, but if you find the chief's arms and take the two principal colors of it, you will usually be right. Just be sure one of the two colors is either gold or silver (yellow or white). Any of these cockades may be in the form of the one you are removing, or a rosette, or a St. Andrew's cross. The last is particularly suitable for the white Jacobite cockade. The appendix gives instructions for making a new toorie or cockade.

THE CLANSMAN'S CREST BADGE

This section appeared in Forebears *and is Copyright 1973 by The Augustan Society, Inc. Reproduced by permission.*

For this section a few definitions will be in order. A circlet is simply a plain circle that furnishes a place to put the motto (see fig. 2a). The wreath is the twisted cloth that looks like a piece of rope at the bottom of the crest. It is part of the crest, appearing in all the brooches we illustrate. It is labelled in figure 2a. "Garter" and "buckle and strap" refer to the same device. The circlet takes the form of a buckled belt, with the end that has passed through the buckle looped around the standing part of the belt (see figs. 2b & c).

Before discussing the development of the crest badge, a few words may be added on another form of the crest. The chief of a clan may wear three eagle feathers behind the cockade that supports his crest. A chieftain wears two, and a *duine uasail* (armiger) one feather. When not wearing actual feathers, these may appear as one, two, or three little silver feathers behind the circlet that bears the motto (see figure 2d). The use of these feathers should be strictly limited to those whose status has been recognized by the Lord Lyon. A common solecism is the wearing of feathers, real or in silver, behind the crest by "chiefs" and "chieftians" of clan societies or other social organizations of Scots and their friends, but this is completely incorrect. A person who bears assumed arms may wear his own crest, with the motto on a plain circlet but no feathers (see figure 2a). The lack of a buckle and strap indicates that it is his own crest and motto, not that of his chief. This is even accepted in Scotland, provided the wearer is not a resident or national of Scotland, and of course provided also that he is not wearing someone else's crest. In the case of alien nonresidents, the Lord Lyon will not assume jurisdiction except in cases of usurped arms.

8

WREATH

Figure 2. Crest and crest badges. a) The crest of a man who has his own arms appears with the motto on a circlet or other plain form of ribbon. The wreath is part of the crest. b) A clansman wears the crest of his chief encircled by a buckle and strap bearing the chief's motto. The buckle and strap is the sign that he does not claim the crest as his own. This converts the crest into a badge. In earlier badges, c), the buckle and strap took the exact form of the insigne of the Order of the Garter. Later ones, b), change the way the end of the strap is tucked in. d) The crest of the Macneil of Barra. The three feathers are the sign of his rank as chief of a clan.

The clansman who has no crest of his own wears his chief's crest on its wreath, surrounded by a buckle and strap bearing the motto. This indicates that it is worn as a clan or family badge and not as the wearer's own crest. The reason for this interpretation of the buckle and strap is said to be that in the old days a retainer would wear his chief's badge on a metal plate buckled to his arm or hanging around his neck with a buckled strap.

So far this is quite clear and straightforward, but when we go back to heraldic authorities at the turn of the century, we find Fox-Davies, author of the classic text, *A Complete Guide to Heraldy*, denouncing the use of the "garter" around the crest by any but Knights of the Order of the Garter:

> In speaking of the garter, the opportunity should be taken to protest strongly against the objectionable practice which has arisen of using a garter to encircle a crest or shield and to carry the family motto. No matter what motto is placed on the garter, it is both bad form and absolutely incorrect for anyone who is not a Knight of the Garter to use a garter in any heraldic display.

This appears to have been confusing to J. P. Brooke-Little, Richmond Herald, when he annotated the recent edition of the Fox-Davies text. His note on this matter reads:

> 243. It may be bad form to encircle the crest with a "garter" carrying the motto, but I doubt if it is "absolutely incorrect", particularly in view of an accepted Scottish custom; for in Scotland Lord Lyon King of Arms allows clansmen to use the chief's crest within a "belt and buckle" inscribed with the motto. The widespread use of these "garters" throughout the United Kingdom suggest that there is nothing too heinously wrong with it.

He might have described the usage as worldwide, since the wearing of the crest badge with Scottish attire is by no means confined to the United Kingdom.

Another authority, Sir Francis Grant, Albany Herald (later Lord Lyon), agrees with his contemporary, Fox-Davies. In his *Manual of Heraldy,* he notes that a badge should properly have neither wreath nor motto (both present in today's crest badge) and adds: "Crests further should not, as is common in crest brooches, be surrounded by a garter, that being the exclusive right of Knights of that order."

It thus appears that the present custom described at the beginning of this article, does not accord with the advice and opinions of experts at the turn of the century. The "explanation" of the clansman's buckle and strap must be relatively recent. Nobody tried to counter the objections of Grant and Fox-Davies with any such explanation. Let us note a few further facts bearing on the problem before we hypothesize an explanation.

Firstly, portraits of chiefs contemporary with Fox-Davies and Grant often show a brooch consisting of a crest, surrounded by a garter with the chief's motto. Specifically, there are the portraits of Norman, 25th, and Norman Magnus, 26th Chiefs of the Clan MacLeod, in Dunvegan Castle, and the photograph of William Harry Hay, 19th Earl of Errol, in *The Highland Clans* by Sir Iain Moncreiffe of That Ilk. All of these were undoubtedly chiefs, yet each portrait shows them wearing the buckle and strap that today is the sign of a clansman. A further interesting example is from another book by Moncreiffe of That Ilk, *Simple Heraldry.* I do not mean to be quoting unduly from the works of a single author; it is only that his works must be the source of a great deal of information for anyone studying Scottish heraldy and the clans. In any case, this example is an illustration by Don Pottinger, Unicorn Pursuivant. It shows a bonnet brooch of Drummond, Earl of Perth, which has both the buckle and strap and the three feathers of a chief.

12

According to today's practice, this would be quite anomalous, but I would be willing to bet, without having verified it, that the illustration was taken from an actual brooch, old enough to predate the explanation that the buckle and strap constituted the insigne of a clansman who was wearing his chief's crest as a badge.

Another perplexing thing is that the old descriptions of retainers wearing their chief's badge referred rather to servants than to clansmen at large. Furthermore, they wore the chief's badge, not his crest, though the two might be similar. However, the badge, as Grant points out, never rests on a wreath, as a crest always should. Finally, I have seen no ancient mention of the wearing of badges that makes any reference to straps or buckles. The badge seems to have been worn suspended from the neck on a chain, or if on the sleeve, embroidered on the garment, just as the Yeomen of the Guard (who are among Her Majesty's retainers) wear the royal cipher (which is a badge, not a crest) embroidered on their uniforms. Any mention of straps and buckles occurs only in explanations of the form of the modern crest badge.

The late Sir Thomas Innes of Learney, Lord Lyon King of Arms (then Carrick Pursuivant) in his book, *Scots Heraldry,* cites the grant of a new seal to the Faculty of Advocates in 1856, to show that the term "belt and buckle" goes back as far as that date. When you look up the citation, the blazon calls the device around the shield "a belt azure, buckled and edged or." This is incomplete, since the blazon does not mention that the end of the belt loops around in exactly the same way as the garter in the insigne of the Order. The citation simply shows, however, that as early as 1856 people were copying the garter insigne and calling it something else.

This is precisely the practice that Fox-Davies and Grant were condeming in their time, half a century later. Furthermore, this usage of 1856 has nothing to do with the modern use of the same device by a clansman wearing his chief's badge. Even the terminology has changed slightly. The device called a "buckled belt" is now usually referred to as a "buckle and strap." It would have been unlikely that a chief's crest would have been worn on his retainer's belt.

A final fact worth noting is that until relatively recently the form of the buckle and strap surrounding the crest badge was identical with the insigne of the Order of the Garter, except for the motto. Latterly, however, the form assumed by the end of the strap that has passed through the buckle has been altered to differ slightly from the knot of the Garter insigne (see Figure 2c).

There is no sure explanation for all these facts, but an hypothesis can at least be advanced for examination. If correct, it would give a complete history of the bonnet badge, consistent with all·the facts we have noted. Here, then, is the hypothesis:

During Victorian times, the custom arose which Fox-Davies and Grant described and deplored. Crests were surrounded with a garter, bearing the family motto instead of the *Honi soit qui mal y pense* of the Order of the Garter. This was done, incidentally, not only on bonnet crests, but on crests for stationery and other uses. People started to use crests to which they had no proper claim on brooches, stationery, and elsewhere. Fairbairn's *Book of Crests* served as a source-book for jewelers, stationers, and others. This is still a very interesting text today, as long as it is not taken as an authority.

Although the contemporary authorities railed at this incorrect practice, it persisted in spite of them. Finally someone rationalized things with the explanation of the "clansman's buckle and strap." This was ingenious enough, but it apparently had no foundation in fact, for early references to the wearing of badges did not mention buckles or straps. The citation from the Lyon Register was adduced, though it did not have any bearing on chiefs and clansmen. It only showed that as early as 1856 the garter device was borrowed under another name. Finally, the form of the buckle and strap was changed to make it less exactly like the insigne of the Order of the Garter. According to our hypothesis, the simultaneous use of the feathers of a chief and the belt and buckle of a clansman had not been considered anomalous, because the latter had not yet been postulated as the sign of a clansman.

None of the above is to be taken as any disparagement of the present usage, which has been accepted for perhaps half a century. We are merely entering a footnote to the history of the development of the present usage. Without taking into account the changes that have occurred, the statements in Grant and Fox-Davies and the evidence of the early pictures can be very confusing indeed. The hypothesis we have presented explains the attitude of Grant and Fox-Davies, as well as showing how the "objectionable practice" of the turn of the century has become the established and honored custom of today.

Sir Crispin Agnew, Rothesay Herald, has pointed out in *The Highlander* (Vol. 26, #3, May/June '88) that any use of this device other than wearing it as a badge—that is using it on anything that could be considered property—is wrong and in Scotland would be illegal. He notes the exception that has been made for its use on writing paper, with the following notation, "Member of the Clan . . ." or the Gaelic *An Cirean Ceann Cinnedh.* The last, incidentally, is not the equivalent of the English; it means, "The crest of the Clan Chief," which is not entirely accurate, since, as we have seen, the crest has been converted into a clansman's badge by the buckle and strap.

TARTANS

A Scottish reviewer said that the Edinburgh edition of this book (May 1981) "could have done with an extra chapter saying something of the origins and controversies surrounding tartan." This section is being inserted to satisfy that demand. I did not do this in the first place, partly because of some unwillingness to become embroiled in those controversies. Also a book like this is no place for an exhaustive study of the tartan. However, going once over lightly may clarify the subject somewhat, leaving the chapter-and-verse studies for weightier books.

Tartan means three things, depending on whether you say "tartan," or "a tartan," or "the tartan." Tartan is cloth: most kilts are made of tartan. A tartan is an identifying symbol: each clan is identified by a tartan—at least one tartan, sometimes several. The tartan is one of the two great symbols of Scotland, along with the bagpipes. In the sign language used by the American hearing-impaired, the sign for Scotland/Scottish is a crossways flick of the fingers against the sleeve, symbolizing the checked pattern of the tartan. The equivalent British sign is a pumping of the left elbow—the bagpipes this time.

Several characteristics identify tartans. They are twill woven—the weft threads go over two and under two of the warp. This gives the diagonal lines of the colors. I doubt that you've come this far without having a piece of tartan where you can put your hand on it, and you can see this feature best in an actual piece of material. However if you have to, you can turn to Plates I and II (facing pp. 32 & 37) where it shows up pretty well.

15

Tartans are doubly symmetrical. The weft is the same as the warp. If you rotate the piece of tartan you are looking at 90°, it will appear unchanged. Also there are two places in each sett—the sett is the pattern of a tartan—where you can put a mirror and see the same thing in both directions. The MacLeod sett in Plate II reverses at the red and the yellow stripes. The American St. Andrew in Plate I reverses at the wide red stripe in the middle and again half way between the light stripes in the blue.

Finally a tartan stands for something. Each clan has a tartan (or several), and some tartans stand for families, so a person may have a family tartan as well as a clan tartan. You may wear them alternately or together (see SHIRT AND TIE, below). Some families not associated with clans still have their own tartans instead. For those with neither a clan nor a family tartan, there are district tartans, as Angus or Galloway in Scotland, or the several Canadian tartans, or our own American tartan.

There are exceptions to all these rules. Particularly for small items like scarves or neckties, you may see tabby weave (plain over-one-under-one). In older setts—there's a famous portrait of Moray of Abercairney dating from about 1735—the warp may not match the weft, and setts that do not reverse (repeating setts) are also not uncommon in the older tartans, particularly those from the islands. The Buchanan sett that is seen so often, probably because it is so colorful with red and yellow, is a repeating sett, but that was a mistake. It was reported by Logan in 1831 as a reversing sett, but the next book that reported messed up Logan's count and came up with the repeating version, which was snapped up by the fashion trade. The record was set straight by D. W. Stewart (*Old and Rare Scottish Tartans*, 1893) but no one paid much attention until his son D. C. Stewart repeated the correction in *The Setts of the Scottish Tartans*, 1950. Then the tartan weavers got it, and you can now get the correct, original, reversing, Buchanan sett as well as the rather garish version we've had all these years.

Finally, you will see "tartans" that don't stand for anything. Some of these are perpetrated by the fashion trade and even given names, like the blue, green, and brown "Bannockbaine," the same sett in three color schemes. There's nothing evil about this sort of thing, and of course it sells yard goods, which is the whole point. Besides, some of the patterns are quite attractive, but why Bannockbaine? If it is a place name, it is not in my Gazetteer, and if it is a family name, it is not in Black's *Surnames of Scotland*.

Other setts that might be said not to stand for anything are "fancy" tartans. A fancy sett is woven for one occasion—a wedding where the whole party is outfitted in the tartan, or a single kilt length. If it is given a name, the word "fancy" will probably be included.

The next question is, "How old is the tartan?" and here the controversy really sets in. When Virgil describes the Celts, after he has mentioned their milk-white skins and golden (by which he meant red-gold) hair, he says, *Virgatis lucent sagulis*, "they shine in striped garments." Now Latin has no word for "checkered." If you look through world-wide vocabularies, you find the only languages with a word for "checkered" are those who play checkers or chess, or some game on a similar board, and the Romans hadn't started to play checkers. And if you couldn't call tartan "checkered," what would you call it but "striped"? So it is not unlikely that among the Celts checkered weaving did go all the way back to Virgil. Enthusiasts say however, "See, they had clan tartans all the way back to Virgil," who was a contemporary of Christ. That, it must be admitted, is driving far past the conclusions that are justified by the evidence.

Incidentally, the word *sagulis* is interesting. *Sagulum* is a diminutive of *sagum*, and the best Latin dictionary the nearest university could turn up for me was a Latin-German, which defined *sagum* as *ein Tuch, ein Reisemantel. Reisemantel* is easy enough: "a travelling cloak," but *Tuch* means, depending on which of two possible plurals you assign to it, "a piece of cloth" or "woolen material." What could be more reminiscent of the *breacan feile* (discussed under PLAIDS, below)?

Several large books have been written about the origin of clan tartans, and the controversy has raged. It was originally claimed, quite seriously, that there had been a fully developed clan tartan system before the '45. Then when the tartan was forbidden all the clan tartans were forgotten. This theory apparently passed over the fact that the proscription only lasted from 1746 to 1782—thirty-seven years inclusive. Many grown men and women at the beginning of the proscription would have outlived it and would have remembered, even preserved pieces of, the clan tartans if in fact they had existed before the '45.

As a matter of fact, there were a couple of incidents during the '45 that showed quite clearly that the tartan was *not* then used as a clan identification. The badge was rather the plant worn in the bonnet. One of the incidents involved two groups of MacDonalds, one Jacobite and the other Hanoverian. The man who described the confusion said you could tell they were all MacDonalds because they all wore heather in their bonnets, and the only way to tell them apart was their black and white cockades. No mention of tartan. Nowadays if you saw a group of MacDonalds at a Games or Gathering, you would say, "They're all MacDonalds—you can tell by the tartans."

The other incident was after Culloden when Cumberland's men were going around the battlefield bayonetting the wounded. They came on a Highlander and were about to finish him off when he said, "Hold your hand! I'm a Campbell." Their reply was, "Sorry, we couldn't tell. You'd lost your bonnet." He was undoubtedly dressed in tartan, or they would not have been bayonetting him for a Highlander, but they couldn't tell he was Campbell without his bonnet and its identifying sprig of bog myrtle. Even if you assume he was wearing hodden grey, they didn't say, "Sorry, we couldn't tell. You weren't in tartan."

Actually right down to the '45 the best evidence is that any time a weaver sat down, he devised a new pattern, as the Navajo rug weavers are said to do today. The only pattern seen repeated is the plain red-and-black check now called Rob Roy. You'd be likely to get this whenever the weaver had just red and black wool and not too much imagination. The portrait of Moray of Abercairney mentioned above, besides showing a differing warp and weft in the jacket, shows a different sett again in the plaid, and this was the rule. When you see a man in two garments of tartan, they will probably be of different patterns. The only exception is in the case of jacket and trews. These would probably be a suit, cut from a single length of cloth. There is a portrait of two MacDonald children at Armadale Castle, and they are sporting five different tartans between the two of them.

During all this time any reference to uniformity in tartan—and they are few and far from clear—nearly always refers to a military unit.

After the '45 the tartan was forbidden, but the proscription was very unevenly enforced. Even after it was lifted, there was no great surge of interest in tartans. That came with the Romantic Revival and specifically with Sir Walter Scott's *Waverley Novels*. It is hard to believe the furor these created. Of course Scott's Highlands were no more like any historical fact than the Wild West of today's TV, but suddenly Scotland was the most romantical place imaginable. Part of this romance was the Great Tartan Myth.

We have already mentioned this myth—that the clan tartans were a thing of great antiquity. We now know that the naming of tartans really got started in the nineteenth century, and a patternbook of 1819 clearly shows this. It was put out by Wilson's of Bannockburn, the most important tartan manufacturer of the time. All of the tartans were listed by number, but a fair proportion had names as well: names of Scottish clans, families, and cities, but also names like Coburg though it was before Victoria had married Albert—even before she had become queen. Being 1819 there was also a Wellington tartan and a Waterloo tartan. The present fate of these named tartans is most enlightening. Only about one in three is still known and used under the same name, though the trade is reviving some of them now, particularly those named for the cities. Most of the rest have simply been forgotten, but a few have been resurrected under new names. Wilson's Coburg is now Graham of Menteith, and his Old Bruce is now MacColl. The plain red-and-green check that Wilson called MacLaughlan was so completely forgotten by 1972 that it was adopted in that year as Moncreiffe.

The only possible conclusion is that in 1819 the business of naming tartans was far from taking any final form—in fact it could be said to have been then in its infancy. Many people will find this conclusion unpalatable. I had a long, heated correspondence when I made the same statement some years ago, with a gentleman who insisted that his tartan went all the way back to the ninth century, at which time it had been an internationally known cognizance all around the North Sea and the Baltic. He said there was documentary proof in the form of a tri-lingual diary, and "who would forge a document to prove a claim about tartan?" For the answer to that question, read on!

Others will object that they have a centuries-old portrait of their then chief wearing the tartan. This would be convincing as a proof of a clan sett only if there were a series of portraits of successive chiefs, all in the same tartan. Unfortunately, when such series exist—and they are far from common—the successive chiefs usually appear in an equally successive series of tartans, and as we have said, if there is more than one tartan garment, the setts usually differ. I know of at least two cases, though, where clans have recently gone to an old portrait and had the tartan copied for clan use. This is perfectly proper, as long as no claim is made that the tartan goes back as a clan tartan to the date of the portrait.

Of course in 1819 people were all trying to discover the ancient clan tartans, which had never existed. Even Sir Walter Scott only denied that the Lowland families had had tartans at any early date, conceding the possibility of early Highland clan tartans. The whole question was complicated by a language barrier. The people being asked the question that had no answer were Gaelic speakers. No wonder the inquiry was not proving successful.

Into this confusion injected themselves two remarkable brothers. They let their friends say—though apparently they never said it themselves out loud—that they were the long-lost grandsons of Bonnie Prince Charlie; that Princess Louisa had gone into the covent, not to escape Charlie, but to have a baby, safe from Hanoverian molestation; and that this child, their father, had been given for adoption to Admiral John Carter Allen. Their father had in fact been adopted and the dates were about right, but no one pointed out that Princess Louisa was still alive in a palazzo on the Lung'Arno in Florence, nor did the young men appeal to her to confirm their story. But no confirmation was needed. People believe what they want to believe, and nobody wanted anything more than they wanted two long-lost grandsons of Prince Charles Edward.

The brothers were accepted and lionized. Their first host, the Earl of Moray, entertained them at his castle, but the Lord Lovat told them to pick their site and he would build them a "hunting lodge." The illustration overleaf is after a detail from an oil painting by John, showing them in this lodge. In size and architecture it would make a nice social hall for a fair-sized church, complete to the hammer-beamed ceiling. John is pointing to the door, where a respectfully saluting gillie is waiting with a brace of hounds.

During this time they underwent a perfect metamorphosis of names. They started as Hay Allan. Their father had changed Allan to the Scottish spelling and adopted Hay because he claimed to be the rightful Hay, Earl of Errol, Lord High Constable of Scotland. The sons soon started calling themselves Stuart Hay and finally Sobieski Stuart (Prince Charlie's mother had been a Sobieska).

It has been necessary to sketch all this because the Sobieski Stuarts published in 1842 the second book with any description of clan tartans (Logan was first in 1831, in an appendix to *The Scottish Gael*). The brothers' book purported to be a description of the tartans of three centuries earlier. It was called the *Vestiarium Scoticum*, and it was a forgery. This has been proved, and it has been

John and Charles Sobieski Stuart, detail from a portrait in oils by the former. The usual costume of the time was the high collar, long coat, and close fitting trousers that you are used to seeing in pictures of Sir Walter Scott and his contemporaries.

proved that the brothers knew it was false when they published it. (See the book I co-authored with D. C. Stewart, *Scotland's Forged Tartans*, Edinburgh, Paul Harris Publishing, 1980, £10.00.) The *Vestiarium* was criticised at the time—Sir Walter Scott said it was a fake—but it was generally accepted; people believe what they want to believe. Controversy continued over the book until the paper I wrote with D. C. Stewart in 1973, though it was not published until 1980. This settled the question both on the substantive basis of what was said about tartans and the stylistic basis of the language, which was what Scott had objected to without documenting his objections.

The *Vestiarium* described over 70 tartans, at least 50 of them being ones the brothers had invented for the occasion. Some thirty-odd of these are still in use today, and there is no point in disparaging them. They are among the earliest of the named clan tartans.

The brothers made some other mistakes, too. One of their passages reads—and this will give a sample of the false language of the *Vestiarium:* yt wes vsit to lay vp intil ylk hovse aine litel wande quharon wes tuinit wollin threidis to the samen nvmber and coulourris as thai suld be wowen to the ylk set in the lom. and quhen that onie wald haue tertteinis of newe thai send the wand vntil the wabster wt as meikle yern as thai had nede that he mycht weaue it lyk vnto the pattron and na mair nor nae lesse.

The source they thought they were following spoke of "a small rod, having the number of every Thred of the Stripe upon it," and the second edition changed "small rod" to "piece of wood." The passage leaves great room for conjecture, but winding the warp takes a lot longer than the actual weaving. When the business of weaving started to be organized, a single weaver could keep several warp-winders busy. Having wound the warp, they would send the skein—which has every thread in order—to the weaver, "twinit" in a figure eight around a small rod or a piece of wood. Furthermore they would also take enough wool identical to the warp for use in the weft, whereas somebody simply ordering a piece of tartan would hardly carry yarn to the weaver. As James D. Scarlett, to whom I am indebted for a good bit of the above, has further pointed out, anyone wanting new tartan from a weaver need only send a sample of the old; there would be no point in the so-called pattern stick, which arose simply from the Sobieski Stuart brothers misunderstanding their source.

Another of their shenanigans arose when they found a genuine reference dated about 1587 and describing a feu duty paid by MacLean of Duart of 60 ells of white, black, and green cloth. Armed with this, they invented the green, black, and white MacLean tartan. Unfortunately they had already completed the first draft of the *Vestiarium*, which they called "a corrupt copy of 1721" (the original, said to date from 1571, was never seen by anyone). A transcript of this first draft was also in the possession of their friend Sir Thomas Dick Lauder. They squeezed the description of the new tartan in at the bottom of a page of their MS and must have persuaded Sir Thomas that it had been missed in making his transcript, for that transcript has it on an added page.

The idea for the book may have been growing for twenty years or so. In 1822 King William IV visited Scotland and the program for the visit was arranged—practically everybody that describes it says "stage managed"—by Sir Walter Scott. He turned it into a very orgy of kilts and bagpipes. Editorials at the time complained that anyone would think everything in Scotland was Highland. The King let it be known that he would appear at a levee at Holyrood House in the kilt, and sure enough he did—Royal Stuart tartan, but with pink tights so that the royal knees were not exposed to the public gaze. This meant, of course, that everyone else had to wear a kilt, and apparently the Sobieski Stuarts let on that they had a secret source describing the ancient setts. We don't know this for sure, but it is of record that several chiefs and other gentlemen got information about tartans from the brothers. Whether they had by this time already written their first draft cannot be shown, but it is not impossible that the date of 1721 scrawled on the first page was exactly a century out. In any event they were passing out tartan information long before they published the *Vestiarium*.

Since the *Vestiarium,* confusion about tartans has not significantly decreased. We have said something about the confusion of color schemes in the section with that title and something of the division of surnames among the tartans in the section *Which Tartan?* We will have more to say below about the confusion arising when a clan has more than one tartan, but from the first there has been the problem of what is the true and authentic sett of any tartan. This is complicated by the fact that no one has ever been able to define what an "authentic" tartan is. The obvious answer is to depend on the decision of the chief of the clan or name. This provides no solution in cases where there is no chief, as with Mac-Tavish or MacFarlane. Furthermore it must be admitted that not all chiefs are experts in the field of tartans. At least a few tartans that have the approval of the respective chiefs betray a less than complete understanding of tartan history or good tartan design.

At the beginning The Highland Society of London depended on the chiefs. They asked each chief to furnish a sample of his tartan with an authentication under his hand and seal. This collection still exists and is of incredible historic value. If it had been kept up to date, it would be definitive now, except for the problems mentioned in the last paragraph.

The Lord Lyon has opened his register to any chief of a clan or name who cares to register a tartan. Unlike the case of arms, there is no requirement that tartans should be so registered. Even with arms, those in use before the establishment of the Lyon Court may continue to be used without reference to Lyon. Many of those bearing such arms have continued to use them so. I may be reading more between the lines than was ever there, but I get the feeling that holders of ancient arms feel a snob value in not having had to petition the Lord Lyon. This may have carried over into the matter of tartans. Whatever the reason, the large majority of the Standing Council of Scottish Chiefs have not availed themselves of Lyon's offer to record their setts.

The Scottish Tartans Society also records the setts of tartans, but they are in the position of dictionary makers. When a tartan has been woven, as when a word has been used, it must be recorded, without regard to whether it is a worthy entry. If a reader or a tartan watcher is likely to encounter it, he is entitled to expect it to be listed. So barring legislation giving control to the Lord Lyon—and it is difficult to see how such legislation could be effectively drafted—we must just struggle along with the situation as it is.

That situation is—in a nutshell—that if you would like to bring a new tartan into being, say a tartan for your family name, all you will need is to design it and send an order for 300 yards (a full bolt) to the Scottish woolen mill of your choice. You will have to send them a thread count, and the Scottish Tartans Society at Davidson House, Comrie, Perthshire, will appreciate it if you send the count to their Monitoring Committee as well. I have been guilty of assisting at the introduction of several new tartans in this way myself.

New tartans have proliferated since the very beginning. My MacTavish tartan—my Scottish ancestor was a MacTavish—seems to date from Victorian times. It was first published in a book in 1906. The Thomson tartans date from the time when Sir Roy Thomson became Lord Fleet. I am told that he specified that one of the supporters he then acquired to his arms should be wearing the Thomson tartan, and they designed not one but two Thomson setts: the azure Dress Thomson and the brown Hunting Thomson, both of them color variants of the MacTavish, which is now also being sold as Red Thomson.

This opens a whole new can of worms—not the Thomson tartans, but the whole new concept of dress and hunting tartans. It probably started right at the beginning. The *Vestiarium* gave the MacLeod tartan as three black stripes on yellow—one of the wildest setts around, and it still is around. When it first came out, someone said, "It would make a lovely horse blanket," so some people have called it the horse-blanket MacLeod. Then another MacLeod tartan surfaced, a much more logical one. It just happens to be the one we have shown in Plate II (facing p. 37). But this left them with two tartans for

MacLeod, and at that stage in the proceedings, when everybody was taking the naming of tartans so deadly seriously, that would never do. The first solution they tried was to make a geographical distinction. The yellow sett was called MacLeod of Lewis and the green one MacLeod of Harris. This didn't help much; apparently people couldn't keep straight which was which. Then someone said, "Well, they couldn't wear the bright tartan hunting; it would scare off all the beasties." So the yellow sett became Dress MacLeod and the green one Hunting MacLeod.

As soon as the MacLeods had a dress and a hunting tartan, everybody else wanted to have the same. Red tartans were converted to a brown background to make a hunting tartan. This harked back to an old reference to brown plaids that would not stand out against the heather, but that reference could as well have meant plain, unpatterned brown. Besides deer and grouse are. color-blind. Red would disturb them no more than brown. Some red setts have been put onto a green, rather than brown, background, and this can be very effective.

Then many of the setts based on the Black Watch were modified by inserting a broad white panel to make a dress version. This proliferated, and broad bands of white have been inserted into many setts. The last batch I saw included this treatment of Hunting Ross and Hunting Stewart of Appin. What are these, then—Dress/Hunting setts?

This points up the fact that "dress" and "hunting" are not very useful terms. You can't be sure whether they refer (as with Thomson) to color variants of the same sett or (as with MacLeod) to two completely unrelated setts. The best answer is to mention the color. Then everyone knows what you are talking about even in a case of proliferation like Scott where you have a red, a brown, and a white sett (color variations of the same pattern) and a totally unrelated green Scott tartan. At least mention the color as well and talk of the yellow Dress MacLeod and the green Hunting MacLeod!

The only case this does not fit is the Black Watch setts with added white. "White Gordon" would not be a very good description of that sett. However, students of tartan have a word for these that we can borrow: arisaid. The arisaid was the ancient women's dress, and the tartans used were principally white. So the modern setts with added white are called "arisaid setts."

This even gets us off the hook on the Dress/Hunting setts mentioned above. We can always say "arisaid Hunting Ross," and it doesn't sound too awful.

This outline of tartans is admittedly sketchy, but a sketch was all we intended. So on to the next section and some advice on which sett you should choose!

WHICH TARTAN?

The first question to settle before you order a kilt is which tartan you want to wear, and the first thing to remember about this question is that most people take it much too seriously. To begin with, there is no such thing as the "right" to wear any tartan. The dictionary definition of rights lists three kinds: legal, moral, and divine (as in "the divine right of kings.") Since it has never been suggested that any use of tartan is illegal, immoral, or ungodly, it is meaningless to talk about anybody's right to any tartan. The whole question is a matter of good or bad taste. Remembering this will help to keep things in their proper perspective.

The "correct" tartan idea was taken very seriously right at the start, in Sir Walter Scott's time, when they started giving clan names to the tartans. Obviously there was not going to be a tartan for every surname, so what of those who had a name for which a tartan had not been designed? A very ingenious theory was advanced, and incidentally it was shot down by serious scholars almost immediately. This was that each clan included, in addition to clansmen who were blood relatives of the chief, "septs" who were incorporated into the clan in spite of the difference of blood, which of course would result in a different surname.

"Sept" is actually nothing but the Irish word for "clan." In old documents where the Scots would refer, say, to "Cameron of Lochiel and all of his name and clan," a similar Irish reference would be to "O'Donnell of Tyrconnel and all of his name and sept." But when the fiction of a non-genealogical "house within a house" was created, they had to have a name for the creature and

29

chose "sept." Of course the ancient clans had no such formal organization. At the height of the clan system surnames were not yet used, and an "incomer" would be a stranger for a generation or two, but then his descendents would be just as much clansmen as anyone else.

We should face the fact that when the rage for clan tartans arose, extra surnames were parcelled out among the clans, sometimes pretty arbitrarily. Historical connections were noted when possible, as the MacCrimmons who were pipers to the MacLeods of Skye, but this was not always possible. I personally prefer to say, "Thomson is a Clan MacThomas or Clan Campbell name," rather than, "Thomson is a sept of Clan MacThomas or Clan Campbell." It is nearer the facts and does not have any flavor of fakery. However my preferences are not going to change so intrenched a Scots usage, and the clan societies will continue to publish and revise "sept lists" of names that belong to the various clans.

One of the most highly regarded of these lists is the chapter, "The Septs of the Highland Clans," in Frank Adam's *Clans, Septs, and Regiments of the Scottish Highlands*. Yet when Sir Thomas Innes of Learney revised this book in 1952, he commented, "This chapter must be regarded as a rather wonderful effort of the imagination." And Sir Thomas was Lord Lyon, King of Arms, the ultimate authority on genealogy and clanship in Scotland. There is nothing wrong with consulting these lists in choosing a tartan. Just don't be surprised if, on a given name, the lists don't agree with each other! No two lists do agree in detail. Incidentally a mistake in an Appendix to the Adam book has been picked up and perpetuated in many other clan lists. He gives at the back of the book an alphabetical list of family names and the clans they belong to. Owing to a printer's error in arranging the lines, Love is given as a Campbell of Loudoun name, Lucas as MacKinnon, and Lyon as Lamont. By comparing with the chapter on septs, one finds that he intended Love to be MacKinnon, Lucas to be Lamont, and Lyon to be Farquharson. However it is probably too late to run down this error and correct it.

The completest listing I know of is *Scots Kith and Kin,* a booklet you can find for sale, or at least available for consultation, in almost any store that will order you a kilt. It boasts over four thousand names and has been decried as an attempt to give a tartan for any name whatever. It also gives a tremendous amount of information without giving a source for any of it, but comparison shows it to be based in large part on Black's *Surnames of Scotland,* which is the ultimate authority on the subject. Unfortunately Black says almost nothing about clans and absolutely nothing about tartans. On the whole *Scots Kith and Kin* would appear to be as useful as any of the other listings. Often it will give only a location, as: "SPEEDIE . . . Dunfermline etc., 16th c." Dunfermline was the capital of the ancient kings of Fife, who were MacDuffs, and this would give a reason for someone named Speedy or Speedie to choose the MacDuff tartan. Of course the MacDuff kings were long gone from Fife by the sixteenth century, but as we said at the beginning, you should beware of taking this tartan business too seriously.

Sometimes the book may give a less helpful area origin, like Glasgow or Midlothian. Glasgow has no particular clan association, and on a clan map Midlothian is a crazy-quilt of little patches. The only names associated with tartans are Stewart, Sinclair, and Kerr, and Midlothian is not really the home base of any of these. In a case like this, in the absence of any family information, you can just pick any of the three and say, "Coming from Midlothian, my forbears are as likely as not to have been dependent on the Sinclairs," (if you picked Sinclair, which has two handsome tartans, one red and one darker).

We probably should have said at the beginning: if you do have any family information or tradition as to clan membership, however remote, it is far better to go by that than to consult any of the name lists. Also any relationship at all is good enough, on your mother's side as well as your father's. Remember no one is talking about rights; all you are looking for is a reason for wearing some tartan that is better than "because I like the colors." If your wife is a clanswoman, her relatives should be flattered and honored if you choose her tartan for your kilt. You might sound them out on the matter first. There are some people who still like to talk about the right to wear a clan tartan and don't realize they are talking nonsense.

If all else fails, and you still don't want to pick a tartan just because you like the colors, there are the "general" tartans. We now have an American tartan. It was designed by James D. Scarlett of Milton of Moy, Inverness-shire, the prominent writer on tartans. Since it came out during the Bicentennial, it was first known as the American Bicentennial tartan. It is now called American Saint Andrew's, having been first adopted by the Saint Andrew's Society of Washington, DC. It was designed for the special purpose of having a sett for Americans who had no particular reason for wearing any of the clan tartans, as well as to provide a choice for a second kilt for any American (See Plate I).

This tartan is hardly a new departure. There is a tartan for each of the Canadian provinces, and Maple Leaf with a white "dress" variant for general use by Canadians. There was also a Canadian Centennial tartan, but it is little used now. And there have always been tartans recommended for those without clan connections. These include the Caledonia (a red tartan) and the handsome green Hunting Stewart. There is also Jacobite, which is principally orange and green, and which most people find less attractive than the others.

Plate II. Three color schemes. The top is the dark "modern" colors, center is the lighter "ancient" colors, and bottom the "muted" or "reproduction" colors. But all three are the same tartan: the green MacLeod.

COLOR SCHEMES

After you have chosen the sett, you are up against the confusing fact that each sett can be woven in any of several color schemes. The major manufacturers have each at least three color schemes, and to make matters even worse, these are not the same from one manufacturer to the next. If at all possible, see a swatch of the material before you order your kilt. In general there will be one color scheme of dark colors, one of lighter colors, and one of muted colors. The way these run in one manufacturer's sample book is illustrated in Plate II, facing p. 37. .

There is a dark color scheme called "modern" and a lighter one called "ancient." The reason for these names involves a bit of history. During Victorian times, it was stylish to use very dark dyes—the blues almost black and the green very dark as well. This made for some very somber tartans and also made recognition less easy in many cases. When they decided to use lighter blues and greens, however, they were not content just to say, "Let's do it!" They had to have a reason. So they argued that with the old dyes the darker colors could not have been produced, and they called the lighter color scheme "ancient" colors. Actually, indigo, which was available from a very early date, gives as dark a blue as anyone could wish. I have also been assured by one or two well meaning salespeople that these lighter colors are produced with vegetable dyes today. This, of course, is not the case; they are simply supposed to resemble the old vegetable dyes. This same manufacturer also has a faded color scheme called "reproduction" colors. It is illustrated on Plate II and discussed below.

Another manufacturer uses the term "O.C." for "old colors" rather than "ancient." This is a help, because some clans have two tartans with completely different setts (the "sett" is the design of a tartan). One of these

34

designs may be believed to be older than the other and be called the "ancient sett." You can imagine the confusion that then arises with the ancient sett in modern colors and the modern sett in ancient colors, etc., etc. This second manufacturer also calls his third color scheme "muted," rather than "reproduction," and both his O.C. and muted schemes have relatively intenser colors. His muted blues and greens are still clearly blue and green respectively.

In discussing these color schemes I am going to let my personal prejudices run riot. The first is in favor of a tartan being recognizable. After all, we wear tartans as cognizances of a clan, family, or district, and an unrecognizable cognizance is about as direct a contradiction in terms as you could find. My second prejudice is against fakery, and this rules out the faded color scheme *ab initio*. This color scheme is supposed to reproduce (hence "reproduction"?) the colors of a tartan that had been dyed with vegetable dyes two hundred years ago and has been fading ever since. The blacks are black and the blues are faded to dove grey. If you ever see a piece of real old faded tartan, the blues are the colors that stay dark, and the blacks go off to an almost khaki color. There is a well known example of this in a tartan bedspread at Blair Atholl in the Murray of Atholl tartan. Besides who would countenance dying a cloth, using permanent synthetic dyes, to look like a long-faded vegetable-dyed tartan? It is esthetically on a par with the Victorian practice of building a "folly", which was a romantic ruin at the bottom of the garden, so that lovers of this generation could do whatever they might be impelled to do in a romantic ruin.

This leaves a choice between the dark "modern" colors and the lighter "ancient" or "O.C." color schemes. With red tartans there is little difference in the ease of recognition. Your choice will depend on whether you like the lighter stripes and more orange red of the "ancient" or the dark stripes on scarlet of the "modern."

With the "blue and green" tartans the difference in recognizing them depends on whether the blues and

Plate I. The American Saint Andrew's tartan. This was introduced during the bi-centennial and was first known as American Bicentennial.

greens come together. If there is a black stripe between them, the light "ancient" colors always show the pattern up more clearly. If not, if the blue and green border on each other (as in Mackay, Gunn, Mathieson, etc.), the "ancient" color scheme blends them together in a way that is very confusing to the tartan spotter. In these the "modern" colors, with the blues perceptibly darker than the greens, provide an aid to recognition.

In all the above I have put "ancient" and "modern" in quotes, because I do not like either term. It is much better simply to talk of the "dark" and "light" color schemes. I realize, however, that people, particularly those in the tartan trade, will continue to talk about "ancient" or "old" and "modern" colors, so I have used the terms in the discussion above.

Just lately (as of 1976) yet another color scheme has been introduced, which the manufacturer calls "blue colors." It is very similar to the reproduction colors, except that the blue (which is grey in the latter) is clearly blue, though still a light, pale blue. Since the green is still brown as in the reproduction colors, the overall effect is bluish, accounting for the name.

I will close by saying what I said at the beginning: these comments on color schemes are my own prejudices, pure and simple. If you are not as insistent on tartan being recognizable (and few people are as insistent as I), or if you admire the lovely soft colors of the "reproduction" scheme, remember *de gustibus non disputandum,* and I am the last person in the world to advance my tastes as authoritative.

One final thing about the choice of a tartan: a man will do well to avoid any of the "dress" tartans that incorporate substantial amounts of white. These were inspired by an eighteenth-century description of Scottish garb which said that the women's dress "called Arisad, is a white Plad." Modern spelling makes this "arisaid", and since these setts were inspired by a women's fashion, the purists do not like to see a man wearing them. This in spite of the fact that many men do wear them, particularly for evening or for competitive dancing.

WHAT ABOUT THE PURISTS?

We have led up to a more general question that will be with us throughout this discussion. There are many cases like this matter of arisaid tartans where there is a definite division of opinion. In some of these cases I will give my own opinion for what it is worth; in others I will simply state both sides of the question or give an opinion as being that of "the purists," with the plain implication that not all authorities agree. My advice to the beginner, though, is to be very careful how you depart from any of these rules. Any variation will probably be laid to ignorance. It will be plenty soon enough to start making individual variations when you are really at home in Scottish attire, after wearing it for several years.

Another question along the same line is that of an American style in Scottish attire. In some ways this makes sense. A Palm Beach kilt jacket is a lot better than heavy tweed for Florida, or for almost anywhere in the United States in the summer. Similarly, lighter weight stockings are sensible, though there would be no need for them in Scotland. But the cut of the jacket and the style of the stockings can conform to the traditional pattern. It is quite another thing when you see evening accessories such as the jewelled dirk or an evening plaid worn with a hairy tweed sports jacket. I try to judge all these things the way my chief, or any Scotsman accustomed to wearing the kilt, would look at them. I am sure he would approve of light-weight jackets and socks for a warmer climate, but I am just as sure that a dirk and evening plaid with afternoon wear would look ludicrous to him. We see this sort of thing much too often in the United States. Once when I was critical of this very combination, I was told, "But I have the dirk and plaid; why shouldn't I wear them?" The answer is that to any intelligent Scot, it makes you look like a lummox. The approximate equivalent would be to wear a tuxedo jacket, black tie, and ruffled shirt with blue jeans and sneakers.

Some people, when I talk like this, call me a purist, but of course I am not. I will not admit to being a purist any more than anyone else will. Nobody considers himself a purist. My position—no matter how strict or how permissive—is the middle of the road. Anyone stricter is a purist, and if he's less strict, he's going straight to the dogs. Kidding aside, though, the beginner is well advised to stick to the rules—even the strictest rules. There's plenty of time later, as we said, for branching out.

AND THE LADIES

While we are digressing, there are two subjects I have been asked to cover that are not strictly concerned with wearing the kilt. The first is ladies' wear. This has nothing to do with the kilt, because no lady is going to wear the kilt. This is not male chauvinism; it is anatomy. The difference between a man's waist and hip measurements is a matter of three or four inches. This remains fairly constant whether the man be fat or thin. Some of this can be taken up where the aprons join the pleats, and the rest, distributed among the two dozen or more pleats, makes the sewn part of the pleats very nearly parallel. Thus it is easy to recreate the pattern of the sett almost exactly in the sewn pleats of the kilt. With a lady the typical difference is a good bit more, and to make up the difference, each pleat must be quite definitely tapered from hip to waist. Thus it is impossible to recreate the sett of the tartan without distortion. I don't know why more ladies' skirts—for the garment we are discussing is a kilt-skirt, not a kilt—are not made with the "military" pleating, with the same stripe down the center of each pleat, but I cannot recall having seen one done that way. I must confess, though, that when I am looking at the back of a lady's skirt, my attention is not always focussed on the sett of the tartan.

I have known one lady who did wear a kilt, but she wore it high up at the "empire" waistline, buckled round her ribs. It was a longish kilt, and she was not a tall lady, so it resulted in an attractive skirt length, not too short. On her it looked good. But by and large the ladies' garment is a kilt-skirt. The length varies from year to year, and I am no expert on ladies' styles, so I will give no advice on this. The purists say that a kilt-skirt, like a lady's jacket, should lap over from right to left, that is with the right apron over the left, just the opposite from the kilt, but you will see kilt-skirts both ways.

One point of ladies' fashions needs to be clarified: there is a great deal of confusion about the wearing of the tartan sash by ladies. Different authorities have said different things, and no one has been able to give a definite answer. The Royal Scottish Country Dance Society has said all along that ladies should wear the sash pinned at the left shoulder, while a more complicated code has been advocated by others. The Lord Lyon has recently approved this more complicated code, but his decision is not binding, and as of the present edition, the R.S.C.D.S. is still holding to its own dictum.

The code approved by the Lord Lyon is as follows: ladies in general should wear the sash pinned at the right shoulder. There are three exceptions, and these should pin the sash at the left shoulder: 1) ladies who are chiefs or chieftains in their own right, 2) wives of chiefs and chieftains, and 3) wives of colonels of Highland regiments. There are also rules as to how to wear the sash. Commonly it is passed under the opposite arm with a bit more of it coming in front than in back. Then the shorter back end is passed over the opposite shoulder and left to hang in front. Finally the longer front end is crossed over the other to hang down in back, and the whole thing pinned at the shoulder. This is shown in figure 3a. A lady who has married out of her clan pins the center of the sash at the appropriate shoulder. The ends are then tied in a bow at the opposite hip. I don't ever recall seeing a sash worn this way, but that is what it says in the book, and we show it in figure 3b. I assume that this applies to a lady who has not married into another clan. Otherwise she should certainly be perfectly correct in wearing her husband's tartan if she chose.

Sometimes it is desirable not to have the sash cross the front of the dress. The book says this is when decora-

*Figure 3. The usual ways of wearing the sash. a) General.
b) A lady who has married out of her own clan.*

tions are worn or for Scottish country dancing, but as an
old country dancer, I can't really see the point of the latter. However any time the lady chooses, it is proper to
wear the sash so as not to cross the front of the dress, except, I suppose, with the lady who has married out of her
clan. The book gives a specific way of doing this, with a
loop at the middle of the sash fastening to a small button
at the waist. The end is then pinned to the appropriate
shoulder, with a bow coming forward and the end hanging in the back. I have seen several other arrangements.

Figure 4. Two ways of wearing the sash so as not to cross the front of the dress. The lady in b) with the sash pinned at the left shoulder is either a chief, or one of the other exceptions, or a R.S.C.D.S. dancer.

The sash can simply be pinned to the shoulder with a bow coming forward and both ends hanging free behind (see fig. 4b). Or if the dress has a belt, one end of the sash can pass under it, with a loop behind between the belt and the shoulder and the other end hanging free from the shoulder, either in front or in back (see fig. 4a).

As you can see, there is a good bit of freedom in how you wear the sash, but the purists feel pretty strongly about some of it, particularly the matter of the right or left shoulder, and it does no harm to go along with them, unless of course you hold with the Country Dance Society. The pin for the sash can be anything you like, though the men's plaid brooch is both a bit heavy and a bit ostentatious. However there are many smaller Highland brooches, and you can always use the same clansman's badge (I refuse to say "clansperson") that is worn on the bonnet.

Strictly speaking, the sash should be worn only with a long, white evening dress, but you will see them with pastel shades and with cocktail dresses. Neither of these looks bad to me, but let me repeat my disclaimer of any expertise in ladies' fashions.

Slightly less formal, but still worn when the men are in black tie, is a long tartan skirt with jabot blouse. Since a lot of the men will be in lace jabot and cuffs, this smacks a bit—to me at least—of unisex, but on this one I certainly don't expect anyone to defer to my whim. You will also see this outfit with a velvet waistcoat very like what Highland dancers wear.

Apart from these and the kilt-skirt almost any woolen garment can be appropriately made in tartan. One nice one, though not often seen, is a tabard, which is plain, loose, sleeveless dress, slit up the sides to the waist, and worn over a slacksuit or a longer dress. Another handy item is a tartan travel bonnet, which lies flat for packing but can be buckled or snapped into shape for wearing.

A final word to the lasses: get your man out in his kilt early and often! You would be surprised how needlessly nervous the neophyte in the kilt can be, and your moral support is worth more to him than anything else could be. So I'll see you both in the tartan early and often, and may you thrive in the wearing of it!

HOW TO ADDRESS YOUR CHIEF

Another subject to cover while we are digressing from the strict discussion of men's Highland dress is the matter of how to address your chief. It is a matter of concern to Americans interested in things Scottish, and it is far too often done wrong. Practically everything covered below is also covered in Debrett's *Correct Form* which is available in most good libraries. There are some points, however, that even Debrett doesn't cover, and the material in that book is spread out over a good many pages. So a summary and selection of the pertinent data may be in order.

Unfortunately the question is not a simple one, since the chiefs of Scottish clans and names run the gamut from esquires to dukes, and the forms are different depending on the rank involved. Furthermore there may be several correct ways of addressing the same person. As an example Col. Sir Donald Cameron of Lochiel, KT. He would not be addressed as Col. Cameron by a clansman, but the choices still remain of "Sir Donald," "Lochiel," and his Gaelic designation, "Mac Dhomnuill Duibh." That last is all right in the salutation of a letter, but don't try to pronounce it. The Dh- represents a sound that does not occur in English or Scots, and even with a Gaelic speaker to imitate, you may have trouble with it. All these forms are correct, and unless you know his personal preference, you would have to flip a coin. He has been kind enough to permit me to tell you that his personal preference is for "Lochiel." His lady is "Lady Cameron."

Several of the easy solutions from American usage do not apply. In the first place "Sir" and "Ma'am" as polite forms of address are not approved by Debrett's *Correct*

Form. According to them, these forms are reserved for royalty. I am sure, however, that if you call your chief and his lady "Sir" and "Ma'am," they will be willing to charge it off to a strange American custom.

Another American custom that won't work is using in the salutation of a letter the form your correspondent signed with. If he signs "John," you start your letter "Dear John," but if he signs "John Smith," you start, "Dear Mr. Smith." The first-name part of this still works, of course. If you are on a first-name basis with your chief, this will carry over into the way you start and sign your letters to him. But a peer signs simply with his title, as "Argyll" for the Duke of Argyll. Nobody however, except a fellow duke, should salute him in a letter as "Dear Argyll."

Finally, your chief is never, never addressed or referred to as "Mr." and you should be sure his lady prefers "Mrs." before you use it of or to her. We will go into detail about this later, but it is one of the commonest mistakes made by Americans in speech and writing, so we mention it now.

After all these warnings here is some good news: once you learn the correct form it can be used in speaking to your chief, speaking about him, or in the salutation of a letter. The address on the envelope should be more formal, and a list of the correct forms for envelopes will be found at the end of this section.

The thing to remember is that the forms described are the ones that are actually used, and there is no reason to feel self-conscious about using them. Your chief may be a charming and affable young man, but if he is "Lord So-and-So," you call him "Lord So-and-So." If you treat him less formally, because you are the head of a multi-national corporation or because you are a man of about his age who thinks formality is silly, you come through to him, or to any other Scot, as purse-proud or ignorant and in either case as a boor. One chief, who for obvious reasons I will not identify, has told me in connection with formality by clansmen, "I might head my letters 'Dear Kinsman' and tail them 'Your kinsman and Chief'

—just to remind them who's who."

The first rank to discuss is the highest and—perhaps therefore?—the most complex. This is that of duke and duchess. The formal "Your Grace" should be reserved for the most formal occasions. According to the Debrett book "Duke" and "Duchess" are correct informal forms, so a letter starting "Dear Duke" or in conversation "Oh, Duchess, have you heard . . ." must be all right, strange though they appear to the unfamiliar American ear. "Dear Duke of Argyll" in a letter is a bit more formal, but not unduly so. Three dukes have Gaelic designations. Argyll is *MacCailein Mor,* Atholl is *(Am) Moireach Mor,* and Montrose is *(An) Greumach Mor.* These translate, "Son (or rather Descendant) of Great Colin ," "(The) Great Murray," and "(The) Great Graham." Obviously the *an* or *am* would be used when speaking of them, but not when addressing them.

After all that complication, we get a really simple form that may be used for nearly half the chiefs and their ladies, including all the Marquesses, Earls, Viscounts, and Lords. These are known and addressed as "Lord _____" or "Lady _____," using of course their titles and not their surnames. Thus the Marquess of Ailsa is "Lord Ailsa," though his surname is Kennedy, and "Lord Strathspey" is so addressed, though he is a Grant. Similarly "Lady Ailsa" and "Lady Strathspey." In most of these cases I am taking the first and last alphabetically. Unless I go into some personal detail, I have not even asked permission to use the names as examples, and in this paragraph, I have not even checked my sources to be sure there is a lady Ailsa or a Lady Strathspey.

Remember not to use a given name after "Lord" or "Lady"! "Lord Ian . . ." or "Lady Mary . . ." followed by a surname is one of the forms of address for children of peers. The forms of address for the children of the various chiefs is too complicated to go into here. If you are interested, it is all in the Debrett book. But remember that Lord George Murray, Prince Charlie's famous general was the son of a duke! If you must use a given name, it comes before the "Lord" or "Lady," in the case of your chief who is a lord and his lady: "James, Lord This" or "Mary, Lady That." George Gordon, Lord Byron, was the full name of the poet. If they had not used his surname, it would have been George, Lord Byron.

Do not use the forms "My Lord" and "My Lady." These are much too formal for general use by anyone except a servant. One final point here: in an informal reference to a peer, it is all right to use his title alone, as "Ailsa has said..." or "Have you ever met Strathspey?" We have done this in fact in the paragraph where we gave the Gaelic designations of the Dukes of Argyll, Atholl, and Montrose.

We now come to knights and baronets, and here, as we saw at the beginning of the article, there is more than one possibility. Taking the alphabetically first example again, you have the theoretical choice between "Sir Ivar" and "Luss" for Sir Ivar Colquhoun of Luss, Bt. In spite of Lochiel's example, the chances are that a knight or baronet will not prefer the use of his territorial title. I discussed this with one baronet who asked me not to use his name, so we shall put his words in the mouth of an hypothetical XYZ, Sir Xerxes Yuill of Zounds. "I often heard my father's friends address him as 'Zounds'," he said. This would have put it at about the turn of the century. "If you ask anyone," he continued, "whether they know Sir Xerxes Yuill, they'll know you mean the chief of Clan Yuill, but if you ask if they know Zounds, they are likely to ask, 'Who's he?' After all it's not a well known name like 'Lochiel'." So it appears that the use of a territorial title may be considered both old fashioned and maybe a trifle familiar, unless you are sure that the particular chief prefers it. It is also true that, with the exception of cases like Lochiel, the territorial title is not likely to be as well known as the rest of the name. In the first example we have taken unoubtedly many more Scots would recognize the name, Sir Ivar Colquhoun, than would recognize who "Luss" is. A further point is that "Luss" does not define the rank. We shall see that chiefs who are esquires are known by their territorial titles. "Sir Ivar Colquhoun," however, is obviously either a knight or a baronet.

There is one peculiarity here. A knight's given name is always used, but not his lady's. It is always Sir Ivar Colquhoun. "Sir Colquhoun" is an impossible form, unless of course Colquhoun were the given name of someone named, for example, Sir Colquhoun Smith. But a knight's lady never uses the given name, except in the case of a peer's daughter, who would use "Lady" with her given name, regardless of whom she married. Sir Ivar Colquhoun's lady is "Lady Colquhoun," and if there ever were a Lady Mary Colquhoun, it would be a peer's daughter who, if she had married a Mr. Smith, would be Lady Mary Smith.

One final point: it is perfectly correct to refer to Sir Ivar as "The Colquhoun." Some sources imply that only The Chisholm should use this form. The fact is that The Chisholm uses this form and no other, but any chief of a clan or name is properly referred to as "The _____" using the surname involved.

We now come to a particularly Scottish form, "of That Ilk," meaning simply "of that same." "Wallace of That Ilk" is just a variant form of "Wallace of Wallace." This means that the English phrase "and others of his ilk," supposedly "and others of his—usually unpleasant—kind," is really quite meaningless. There is one case where "of That Ilk" is preferred: when the surname is also the name of a territory or estate that is not owned by the chief. A case in point is Sir Iain Moncreiffe of That Ilk, Bt., who owns and lives at Easter Moncreiffe, while Moncreiffe itself is held by his cousin. She is therefore Miss Moncreiffe of Moncreiffe, while he—to give him his full title, which is seldom used—would be Sir Iain Moncreiffe of That Ilk and Easter Moncreiffe, Bt.

In speaking of or addressing Wallace of That Ilk, you call him simply "Wallace," and the salutation in a letter is "Dear Wallace." This may sound a bit unusual, but you are not calling him by his surname, as you would a butler or private soldier. The form you are using is exactly the same as when you address Cameron of Lochiel as

"Lochiel." You address him by what follows "of" in his full name, and obviously you can't say "Dear That Ilk." But the "Wallace" you are using is not his surname; it is the "Wallace" that is represented by "That Ilk" that follows his surname. Thus it is a form indicating respect rather than undue familiarity.

With a knight or a baronet, as we saw above, "Sir" with the given name is more common. It is not technically wrong to address Sir Iain Moncreiffe of that Ilk as "Moncreiffe," but "Sir Iain" is much more usual and normal.

The final category of chiefs are technically of the rank of esquires, but the term is seldom or never used. It is not actually incorrect to say Andrew MacThomas of Finegand, Esq., but it is quite unnecessary. The territorial designation of "of Finegand" after his name, taken with the lack of "Sir" before "Andrew" clearly establishes his rank, so the addition of "Esq." is redundant. The same is true of the chief of a name. Ninian Brodie of Brodie is clearly of the rank of esquire. As we said above, the proper form of address is what follows "of." These chiefs are addressed as "Finegand" and "Brodie" respectively. Remember too they are never styled as "Mr." at least not in clan matters. Finegand is active in the business world and in the line of business will respond when addressed as "Mr. MacThomas," but for a clansman to address him so, or Brodie as "Mr. Brodie," is discourteous if not downright insulting.

There is a bit of a problem with ladies of such chiefs. Technically they are entitled to the prefix of "Lady." Since this has been taken over by the ladies of knights (who technically should be "Dame"), many of these ladies do not use it. The choice is then between "Madame" and "Mrs." If you do not know which the particular lady happens to prefer, you cannot be sure to be right. It is probably better to err on the side of formality and use "Madame." Remember that "Alan Mac-Tavish of Dunardrie and Madame MacTavish" does not refer to a married couple! Her surname is MacTavish of Dunardrie just as much as his is. The late Innes of

Learney, Lord Lyon, in his excellent introduction to *Tartans of the Clans and Families of Scotland*, says that if a couple registered in that way, "any respectable hotel would be justified in turning them out!"

If you are a Macpherson or have occasion to address their chief, you have a special problem. he is Cluny-Macpherson, and you will hear him addressed as "Cluny." This sounds as though people were using his first name, because of course you can't hear the hyphen. As a matter of fact his full name is William Alan Macpherson of Cluny-Macpherson and Blairgowrie. Going by the rules we have given, you would call him "Cluny-Macpherson" and start a letter "Dear Cluny-Macpherson." It would not be incorrect to do so, just a bit cumbersome. So "Cluny" is commonly used as an abbreviation for "Cluny-Macpherson," and you call him "Cluny" and start a letter "Dear Cluny." His lady is "Lady Cluny."

We said we were not going to discuss the forms for children of chiefs, and the correct forms for the children of peers are all in the Debrett book. You do need to know, however, one particularly Scottish form for the heir to a chiefship. To illustrate this we will revert to our hypothetical Sir Xerxes Yuill of Zounds and postulate an elder son, Xenophon. His correct title is Xenophon Yuill, younger of Zounds. He may occasionally write this in a less correct form because it is also less confusing to the uninitiated: Xenophon Yuill of Zounds, Younger. He is referred to as "younger of Zounds" or simply as "young Zounds." These forms are the same for the son of a chief who is not a peer, whether he is a baronet, knight, or esquire.

In closing a letter, there is a centuries-old formula that many chiefs appreciate: "Your loyal and devoted kinsman" or some similar wording. If you are on a more informal basis with your own chief, the Saxon equivalent of "Yours sincerely" is "Ever yours," and there is a nice Scottish variant, "Yours aye."

If a duchess in her own right were chief of a clan or name, she would be addressed like any other duchess, as described above. Peeresses in their own right are addressed just like peeresses who are the wives of peers. So if your chief is a marchioness, countess, or viscountess, she is "Lady. . ." using her title, not her surname. The feminine equivalent of "Sir. . ." is "Dame. . .," and Dame Flora MacLeod of MacLeod was addressed as "Dame Flora," using her christian name, just as a knight would. If the lady is the equivalent of an esquire, the practice is as with an esquire, except that the use of Madam(e) is possible, where Mr. is not. Madam MacDougall of MacDougall is addressed as "Madam MacDougall." In the case of an unmarried lady, "Miss" would imply the eldest daughter of an esquire, so Marian Campbell of Kilberry is addressed and referred to as Kilberry.

It remains only to give the correct form of envelope address for each of the different ranks, again for the alphabetically first of each rank:

H.G. The Duke of Argyll
H.G. The Duchess of Argyll
Most Hon. The Marquess of Ailsa
Most Hon. The Marchioness of Ailsa
Rt. Hon. The Earl of Airlie
Rt. Hon. The Countess of Airlie
Rt. Hon. The Viscount of Arbuthnott
Rt. Hon. The Viscountess of Arbuthnott
Rt. Hon. The Lord Forbes
Rt. Hon. The Lady Forbes
Sir Ivar Colquhoun of Luss, Bt.
Lady Colquhoun of Luss
Dame Flora MacLeod of MacLeod
Ninian Brodie of Brodie
Madame Brodie of Brodie
Madam MacDougall of MacDougall
Marian Campbell of Kilberry

The only catch is that Madame Brodie is technically entitled to be called "Lady Brodie" and may prefer it, or she may prefer "Mrs. Brodie of Brodie." The safest form, unless you know her personal preference, is "Madame."

THE KILT

Firstly the name. "Kilt" is a verb as well as a noun. It means "to gather into vertical pleats like a kilt." One immediately wonders whether the garment took its name from the verb, but it did not. The verb in this sense is not nearly as old as the noun:

Forgive me next for insulting your intelligence, but I have seen this done wrong: the pleats of the kilt are the back of it, and the unpleated "aprons" cross over each other in front, the left-hand apron outside. If you see a garment with the right-hand apron outward, it is a lady's kilt skirt. It used to be common to have an arrangement that you might find useful if you wear the kilt for a work outfit. This is to have it so that either apron can be worn over the other. Then while there is risk of soiling the kilt, the right-hand apron is exposed, but when appearances count, the soiled apron is hidden under the other, which has been kept clean.

When you take the big step of ordering your first kilt, there will be few problems as to the style. Any reputable kiltmaker will fit you out with a kilt you will be proud to wear. I am assured that no reputable kiltmaker will use a kilt length of under eight yards, but I have measured many kilts—some by the most reputable makers—that have scarcely six yards in them, and only the most skilled eye can tell the difference. So don't make an issue of the yardage! Many other things about the kilt are much more important.

The first important point is the material. Unless you are very specific in ordering, the kilt is likely to come through in a lightweight saxony. This is a soft material that does not wear as well nor hold its shape and its pleats as well as worsted. Insist on worsted, even though the initial cost may be more!

The burning issue, however, is the length and how to determine it. In the time of Queen Victoria the kilt was supposed to come to the middle of the kneecap. This is now horribly out of date, but one still sees too many kilts at that length. Some of the old-line kiltmakers are still measuring customers for the longer kilt, so be sure you do not get your first kilt too long! This is particularly important if it is going to be your only kilt. A good kilt will long outlast the wear that most American Scots are likely to give it.

At the very longest, the kilt should reach only to the top of the kneecap. You need not fear that the short kilt is a passing fad. The kilt has often been worn shorter, and the mid-kneecap length was itself an extreme fashion and one we should be happy to see the last of. The most felicitous description of it that I have heard calls it "trollopy."

Don't get the kilt too short, either! One of the books tells of a Highland gentleman who has his heavy kilt that he wears for shooting and hillwalking three inches above his knee. That way it does not touch the calf of his leg at all. That may be all very well if you are going to have a kilt specially for outdoor sports, but for a general-purpose kilt an inch above the top of the kneecap is probably as short as you will want to go, even if you like a shortish kilt. You can change the height of a kilt a good bit by how tight you take up the straps. The tighter you pull them, the more the kilt rides up over your hips at the waist and the shorter it gets. There are limits, of course, and you will find it even easier to slack off the straps and let the kilt ride lower and longer. This is one more reason to be sure you measure on the short side rather than the long.

A lady of my acquaintance, having read thus far in the matter asked, "But if the kilt is too long, why not just take up the hem a couple of inches?" I hope that most of my readers will not need to be informed that there is no hem to a kilt. The bottom of the kilt is the selvedge of the cloth. It is possible to shorten a kilt as described in the appendix (p. 107) but it is a tricky bit of work, not to be undertaken lightly. Still it can be the saving of a kilt you might otherwise be unwilling to wear.

The next question is how to measure to the top of the kneecap. It was quite simple to measure the long Victorian kilt. The wearer knelt down, and the bottom of the kilt should then just clear the floor. This is no good any more as it results in the "trollopy" Victorian kilt. Furthermore kiltmakers and other experts in Scotland get very heated at the suggestion that anyone should check the length of a kilt by kneeling. I don't quite know why, and I can't seem to convey to them the difficulty the beginner has in determining just when a kilt is hanging to the top of the kneecap.

I have three kilts as I write this, and one of them is about an inch shorter than the others. I have always liked the short one best, and it looked to me as if it hung just about to the top of the kneecap. However, in experimenting for this write-up, I marked my kneecap by putting a garter on just at the top of it. To my considerable surprise I found that the longer kilts were just about at kneecap length and the one I liked came about an inch above the top of the kneecap. Now I have worn the kilt probably as often as twice a week for the last ten years and more. If with that much experience, I had difficulty judging the length of a kilt, I certainly can't tell a beginner, "Just wear your kilt at the top of the kneecap!"

Of course the problem is a bit different. What we need is to measure a person for his first kilt. The critical measurement is the one from the lower edge of the kilt straps to the bottom of the kilt. It should be taken from the peak of the hip-bone to the level of the top of the kneecap. You can do this exactly if two people help. One needs to hold a straight-edge across the kneecaps, and the other measures down from the hip-bone to it. If you measure from the hip-bone to the kneecap, the tape will spiral around the leg and the measurement will come out too long. Unless you are dealing with a pretty massive thigh, though, this will not come to over a quarter or a half an inch, and you can allow for it. Don't try to give kilt measurements closer than the nearest half inch, anyway! The kiltmaker does not work to any closer tolerances. And let me say again, keep this measurement on the short side!

If you insist on a kneeling measurement, measure from the hip-bone to the floor and subtract at least two-and-a-half inches!

The only problem with the waist and seat measurements is how tight to make them. The seat measurement should be around the largest part of the seat, and it should be taken over the shirt only, as this is where you wear a kilt. It should not be loose, but neither should it be too snug. The waist measurement, however, should be taken as tight as you plan to wear the kilt. It must be tight enough to hold up the kilt, and if you normally wear your trousers belt fairly tight, pull the tape equally tight when you take the waist measurement for the kilt! This measurement is better too small than too large. You can readily slack off the straps a hole to gain an inch, but taking up an inch involves moving the kilt straps, which is no minor job.

The final measurement is the total height of the kilt. It used to be the fashion to use a full single width of tartan in the kilt. This meant that, particularly with a short man, the top of the kilt would come way up over the short ribs. Worn with a belt, there would be a considerable band of tartan showing over the top of the belt. This is no longer the style. It is preferred now for a belt, when worn, to fully cover the top of the kilt. This is particularly desirable with black-tie evening wear. The fronts of either pleated or ruffled evening shirts are long enough to cover the whole front, down to the top of the kilt. Then a black belt and silver buckle covering the top of the kilt will serve in place of a waistcoat (See fig. 8a). For this to work out, the total length of the kilt must not be over two inches more than the measurement we started with—from the hipbone to the bottom of the kilt. It can well be less; an inch and a half more is plenty. This may mean that the top of the belt will be higher than the top of the kilt, but the shirt will blouse out to fill this space perfectly well.

There are a couple of things that you will have to specify in your order. The first is the manner of kilting. There are two basic ways of pleating a kilt. In one the pattern of the tartan is re-created across the back where the pleats are sewn in. That is, a whole repeat of the sett in the tartan is hidden in each pleat. This is probably what you will get if you don't specify anything about pleating. The other style is known as military pleating. In this style, which you can see in any bandsman's kilt, the same stripe is centered on every pleat. The back of the kilt shows a relatively even color effect, with bands running horizontally, but the pure squares of at least one major color are hidden in the pleats. Thus when the wearer moves in walking or dancing, the hidden color shows in flashes. This can be a very attractive effect. You do not have to be a soldier to wear the military style. It is just called "military" because the army kilts are all pleated so. Look at some kilts pleated both ways and decide which you prefer! My personal preference for the military pleating is probably quite obvious by now, but don't let that influence you unduly! And of course if you pick a tartan like the brighter Oglivie sett, which is forty-seven inches or so to the repeat, you will have to trust the tailor to come up with some sort of a compromise pleating.

Another thing is the number of straps. Any kilt is held up by two straps, one at each end of the top of the unfolded kilt. The one that fastens over the left hip goes through a "buttonhole" in the kilt to anchor the top corner of the under apron. The other fastens the top corner of the side with the fringe to a buckle over the right hip. Some tailors add a third strap at the right side a few inches down. This has the advantage of holding the top, sewn portion of the kilt better in place even during the most violent spins in either dancing or throwing the hammer. A possible disadvantage is that, even when most carefully adjusted, it tends to pull the squares of tartan at the top of the apron a little askew. This is particularly true of those of us who are unfortunate enough to have a slight "pot" under the top of the kilt.

There is a solution to this problem that I saw on a very old kilt, and have used on all of my own. This is to have the third strap on the left, at the same height as the normal right-hand strap. This of course necessitates a second buttonhole on the left, but that is no real problem. The third strap on the left has the same advantageous effect as on the right of keeping the top of the kilt under better control. At the same time, it lets the outer apron of the kilt hang perfectly free. However, when you try to order a kilt with this arrangement of straps, you may have a hard time. It took two confirming letters to persuade a Scottish kiltmaker that I really wanted a kilt with straps this way.

A good worsted kilt seldom needs pressing. And if you can find a cleaner who can press one, even at so much a pleat, consider yourself fortunate! When you do have to press one—as when you have worn a wet kilt in a car— you start by pressing the inside fold of each pleat individually. Then lay the kilt up on the ironing board, and you should be able to press in several pleats at a time.

Usually, though, when you take the kilt off, you just fold it up double inside out, double it again, and hang it in a kilt hanger (what your wife calls a skirt hanger). If you get home too debilitated to do this, spread the kilt over the back of a sofa, with the pleats as accurate as they will lie. For travel it will go well on the same hanger in a flight bag or the like. You can also roll a kilt for packing. If you don't have a mailing tube big enough to slip it into, it may be slid into a silk stocking, which is even easier to pack. Where to get a stocking is your problem.

JACKETS

First off, remember that you don't necessarily have to wear a jacket with a kilt! On informal occasions and depending on the weather, shirtsleeves or a sweater are perfectly all right (See fig. 5b). For heavy work (including sports) in hot weather, you will peel to your T-shirt or to the skin. But on any even slightly formal occasion, where you would wear a jacket if you were in trousers, you will want a jacket with your kilt.

In Scotland you would get a break, because you could go to a surplus store and buy one of the obsolete combat jackets which does very well for informal occasions when the Saxons are wearing sports jackets (see fig. 6b). You might even be able to find one of these jackets in a surplus store over here. Be sure to remove any insignia! Nothing looks sillier than a civilian wearing sergeant's stripes or the crowns and pips of an officer. Failing a combat jacket, you will have to order a kilt jacket and your choice is limited. To be really fully outfitted, you should have two day jackets. The first is the heavy, tweed jacket that most people think of when you say "kilt jacket." Since this is a slightly informal style, appropriate when the Saxons are in sports jackets, we will call it a "sports jacket," though Scottish tailors do not use that term (see fig. 5a). For those occasions that would call for a business suit, the jacket should be of a darker color and a smoother material. For really formal occasions, where the Saxons are in striped pants and cutaway, it should be black and have silver buttons and be worn with a matching waistcoat and evening belt (see fig. 7a). It is also perfectly correct with the black belt alone.

Figure 5. Informal wear. a) The usual kilt jacket is an informal style, like a sport jacket. b) The kilt does not necessarily require a jacket. A sport shirt or, as here, a sweater are perfectly proper on occasion.

This gives the only real opportunity for an all-purpose kilt jacket: black with changeable buttons so that they can be either black or silver. For normal daytime wear, use the jacket without the waistcoat and with the black buttons! Then for evening: silver buttons and black tie. You can dress it up further with a ruffled shirt and/or an evening belt and/or waistcoat. This is a bit dressy for some daytime occasions and not awfully dressy for evenings, but it will get you by. You should not button your jacket—particularly if you are wearing a belt—unless you are putting a coat or a cape over it. Of course if expense is no object, or after you have spent years in building up your wardrobe gradually, you will have a sports jacket, a light day jacket, a Prince Charlie for evening, and some kind of a doublet for full dress, but this is a target for the indefinite future.

Don't settle for a Saxon suit jacket with a kilt! It will be much too long and will look very sloppy indeed. The bottom of the jacket will hang down over the unsewn part of the kilt pleats, which should always be left free to swing. Don't overlook the possibility, though, of having a Saxon jacket cut away and shortened! The appendix (page 108) shows just how to do this, and any competent tailor can handle the job. You don't need shoulder straps or fancy cuffs. These are both relics of a military style. The three-peaked cuff was where an officer wore the crown and/or pips that indicated his rank, and shoulder straps, too, are found on almost all military jackets. There is no real reason, though why a modern kilt jacket should have either shoulder straps or special cuffs. The only exception is a dress jacket you are going to wear with an evening plaid. The shoulder strap is then practically a necessity for anchoring the plaid at the shoulder.

In Scotland you will never see a kilt jacket with a badge on the pocket. If you get one here, it should not have the arms of the chief on it. You can get such jackets, but if you wear one in Scotland, it is illegal and could subject you to a fine and confiscation of the jacket. Here it is simply in the worst of bad taste. This is talking about the whole arms with the shield, crest, helm, and supporters, if any. The crest within a buckle and strap is another matter. You wear it on your bonnet in silver, and it is correct, heraldically, to wear it on the pocket of a

Figure 6. Two styles derived from the military. a) The day doublet resembles an officer's blouse, lacking the skirts and worn with a kilt belt. It can be in any color. b) This is simply the obsolete British combat dress jacket. If you can pick one up, it goes very well with the kilt.

jacket as well. It is not a Scottish style, but it does not look bad to most Americans.

A recent style in Scotland gives you a break, as it requires much less complex tailoring than cutting away a Saxon jacket. This new style is the "day doublet," which is a close fitting, waist-length jacket with military pockets, shoulder straps, and cuffs like a Prince Charlie jacket (see fig. 6a). Try the thrift shop on the nearest army post for an army officer's uniform blouse (as the army calls it), have it cut off at the waist and the skirts used to make a waistband and cuffs! Instructions for this are found in the appendix at p. 108. This will look well enough in the original color, but if you can find someone to dye it without shrinking it, that will make it even better. Any color will do, though it will have to be pretty dark unless you are lucky enough to have located one of the old tropical worsted jackets in the khaki color. The day doublet is for more formal day wear, and can be fitted with plastic buttons in an appropriate color. With silver buttons and black tie, you can even get away with it for evening.

Another currently popular jacket style is known as the *peitean,* which I have been told is simply the Gaelic for "waistcoat." It was developed by Dr. Reginald Hale, F.S.A.Scot. of Ottawa and is particularly suitable for wear in hot weather. it is sleeveless with epaulettes similar to those on a piper's tunic, but smaller. There is a version in black with silver buttons for evening, and it also comes in tweed or even leather for day wear (see fig. 7b).

Your best bet for evening also involves a minimum of tailoring. If you go to a tuxedo rental store, you can often pick up a tail coat (the kind worn with white tie) very reasonably. Try right after the new year when they are likely to have inventoried their stock and put aside the coats that show the slightest signs of wear. They won't look worn; I have been wearing one for over ten years and it still looks new. The tails should be cut off just where the sewing of the pleats in the kilt ends. No kilt jacket should come down far enough to hinder the free swing of the unsewn portion of the pleats in the kilt. The cuffs and the additions to the tails should be copied from a Prince Charlie coatee borrowed from a friend. Or follow the instructions on p. 108 in the appendix! Don't

a *b*

Figure 7. Two daytime styles. a) Black jacket and waistcoat with silver buttons are very formal day wear—like striped pants and cutaway. b) The peitean *is a recent revivial, very convenient for hot weather. It is often worn with a shirt in Colonial style. This style of sporran is also a revival of an old type.*

worry about the shoulder strap or cord! Many Prince Charlies lack them altogether and do perfectly well without them.

The shirt, tie, waistcoast or cummerbund, and other accessories with the Prince Charlie are precisely the

Figure 8. Evening wear. a) The Prince Charlie Coatee is the simplest evening jacket. It is most appropriate with black tie and may be worn with either a waistcoat or evening belt. The inset shows a patent-leather evening shoe with silver buckle. b) A more formal style. The high necked doublet sets off the jabot, and the accessories include dirk and evening plaid. The "Mary Jane" evening shoes are a standard Scottish style—uniform dress in some of the Highland regiments.

same as for any tuxedo. Footwear for evening is discussed elsewhere. Another option with the Prince Charlie coatee has already been mentioned. With most tuxedo shirts you can wear a black evening belt with silver buckle instead of a waistcoat or cummerbund (see fig. 8a).

Some wear full-scale evening accessories with the Prince Charlie: lace jabot, jewelled dirk, evening plaid, and the works. I don't hold with this myself. The jabot does not look well except coming out of a high collar, and the Prince Charlie coatee looks best with black tie and plain accessories.

Kilt jackets for full-dress evening (where the Saxons are in white tie and tails) are mostly called doublets, but that is all you can say about terminology. I have two different booklets each from a leading producer of Highland evening wear, and the identical doublet—single-breasted, with short flaps all round below the belt—is called "Montrose doublet" in one and "Kenmore Doublet" in the other. The one that calls it "Kenmore" give a "Montrose" that is double-breasted and does not come below the belt at all. This is a double-breasted version of what the other book calls an "Argyll doublet" (see fig. 8b). Don't try to follow all that! I am simply pointing out that the naming of evening jackets leads to utter confusion. So before you order one, see a picture in the catalog of the company that is going to supply it, or order it by describing the following points: 1) collar either high so as to take a jabot or with lapels; 2) single-breasted, double-breasted, or cutaway; 3) flaps, which may be: a) lacking—the evening belt covering the bottom of the jacket; b) short all round as in the Montrose alias Kenmore we mentioned above; c) cat tails and Inverness flaps as in a piper's tunic.

The double-breasted doublet will always have a high collar and no flaps, but almost any other combination is possible, as may be seen from the illustrations. One style I personally don't like is the so-called standard or regulation doublet. This is like a Prince Charlie, but has the cat tails and Inverness flaps. It would look well enough with a white tie, as it was usually worn in Victorian

Figure 9. Evening wear. a) The standard or regulation doublet is worn with white waistcoat and tie. A white shirt front does NOT set off a jabot at all well. Castellated hose must be worn with tied garters. b) The Sheriffmuir doublet, worn with a breacan feile. This makes a very ornate evening outfit, fullest of full dress.

times (see fig. 9a), but a white shirt front does not set off a jabot at all well. This style does less to exaggerate the lack of a waistline than most of the other doublets, but if you have this problem, a better solution is the Sheriff-muir doublet (see fig. 9b). This has the high collar and then cuts away in front and has cat tails and Inverness flaps. If you go in for jackets that are tailored from available ones, you can have a Sheriffmuir jacket made, starting with a uniform jacket like the U.S. Marines' officer's mess dress jacket. Take off the gold braid and borrow a piper's tunic for the tailor to follow in the cuffs, tails, and flaps!

Doublets, especially the tight fitting ones, may be made in velvet, and you will see all colors except yellow and orange. They are also made in tartan. The buttons are silver and may be considerably larger than the square or diamond-shaped ones worn with the Prince Charlie. Any time I say "silver," I mean metal. Rhodium plate, which does not tarnish, is currently popular, cut steel is always an alternative, and even gold is not unheard of.

Only one point to remember in ordering any of the tight fitting doublets: your waistline may expand. If it does, you can have the seams let out at the sides a certain amount, but only if there has been plenty of material left along the seam. Chalk up one more point in favor of the Sheriffmuir: if you put on half an inch in your neck, you can always ease the collar fastening some way, and your jabot will hide the trickery.

A final point about doublets or any other jackets: get them in the lightest weights available. If you have never checked it out on a globe, it may surprise you to know that Scotland lies in the same degrees of north latitude as Labrador. Of course the Gulf Stream gets in its good work, so that there are palm gardens at Poolewe, but most of the United States lies in far more southern latitudes. Washington, D.C. is in the same latitude as the Mediterranean coast of Algeria, and Charleston is as far south as the Sahara desert. It is surprising how comfortable a kilt can be in summer, and this is confirmed by those who have worn it in the tropics. But the same is not true of the usual kilt jacket. Even formal attire in Scotland is usually worn in halls much less overheated than ballrooms in the United States. So you will be well advised to get much lighter weight material for all your jackets than is customary in Scotland.

You will see jackets of tartan, but (except for the very occasional tartan doublets and waistcoats for full-dress evening wear) these are not Scottish attire. They are simply Saxon jackets made out of tartan, and there's nothing wrong with them. Just don't expect to see them discussed—except to be mentioned and dismissed—in a book on wearing the kilt.

There are tartan waiscoats, too, and they can be tailored reversible, with the family tartan on one side and the clan on the other. But these are for wear with a Saxon sport jacket and slacks.

Slacks are made in tartan, and the salesman probably called them "trews." The original trews were the alternative to the kilt or the *breacan feile* (see p. 77, below) when you got a horse. The kilt is obviously not suited for wear on horseback. The trews were almost skin-tight, of tartan cut on the bias, and included a covering for the foot, worn inside the shoe. Today trews are an item of military uniform: the very slender trousers some regiments use. Neither of these types of trews is an item of modern Scottish civilian wear, so we only mention them here.

Tartan slacks are simply slacks made out of tartan, and neither this fact nor calling them "trews" brings them under the heading of Scottish attire. I have even seen a pair of tartan tuxedo slacks, complete with satin braid down the seam. They were in the yellow MacLeod tartan, too—really tasteful. If the man had felt like it, he could have had the jacket out of the tartan, with black satin lapels, too. He might even have thought this would make it proper Scottish evening wear.

BELTS AND WAISTCOATS

The trend today is for waistcoats to be worn less and less and belts more and more. We have even seen that an evening belt can replace the waistcoast with the Prince Charlie coatee, and the same is true of any evening style that shows the top of the kilt. And of course the evening belt should be worn with any tight-waisted evening style. An evening belt must be black, of either patent leather or morocco, with a silver buckle, with or without stones set in it (see fig. 10). Evening waistcoats, if you want one, come in black (matching the lapels of the jacket), white, red, or tartan cut on the bias. Some people object to tartan except in kilt or plaid, and others say that a red waistcoat is too reminiscent of footmen. My personal preference is for an evening belt in place of a waistcoat on all occasions.

The only day wear that needs a waistcoat is the dark jacket, and the waistcoat should be matching. A waistcoat is superfluous with a sports jacket. Wear one if you like, but if cost is a consideration, don't bother getting a waistcoat with your tweed kilt jacket!

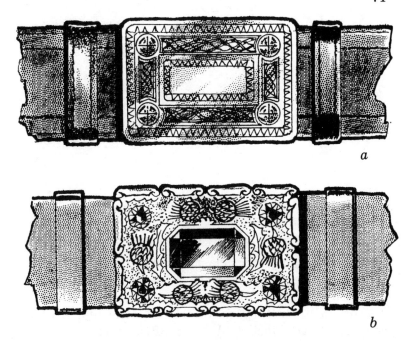

Figure 10. Evening belt buckles. a) Plain silver. b) Set with stones, usually cairngorm.

Belts are now being worn any time one chooses. The black evening belt may also serve with the dark day jacket. If you wear a belt, day or evening, with a waistcoat, the waistcoat should not show below the belt. If the waistcoat is cut with points that would come down too far, simply put your kilt on over the waistcoat. Then the belt will hide the joining as it should. With the sports jacket or any less formal wear—sweater, shirtsleeves, etc.—the black belt with silver buckle is too dressy. The belt should still be wide, 2-1/4 to 3 inches, but the buckle should be brass. Some of the older books call the sport outfit "hunting attire" and insist it should not show any bright metal for fear of alarming the game. If you want to humor those who feel so, you could have the buckle of antique brass rather than polished metal. The belt is better brown than black, to avoid confusion with the evening belt.

SHIRT AND TIE

The only item in this classification that is different in style from Saxon men's wear is the lace jabot and cuffs that are worn with full dress. The cuffs may be attached to the shirt, or they may fasten to the inside of the sleeves of the jacket. I have already expressed my preference for limiting the jabot to wear with a high-collared jacket, but you will see it worn with the Prince Charlie coatee, and even some of the tailor's books show it this way. The only time I would suggest doing this would be when attending a strictly white-tie affair if one did not have a more formal jacket. Even then, I would rather see white waistcoat and tie with the Prince Charlie.

Aside from the jabot, shirts and ties are much the same as for Saxon wear. When turtle-necks are in style, there is no reason not to wear them with a kilt jacket, always maintaining the proper degree of formality or informality. For a picnic, wear a sports shirt—whatever you would be likely to wear if you were not in a kilt. The only thing to avoid is a checkered shirt, which would probably not go well with the tartan of your kilt. Purely anathema (and for me this includes a lady's dress on a Scottish occasion) is something that looks like a tartan but isn't. These are known to Scots as "bumbee" tartans.

Some authorities say you should never wear a tartan tie with a kilt. Other authorities suggest wearing your mother's tartan in a tie (or plaid, described later) and your father's in the kilt. Personally I do not care for a tartan tie with the kilt, specially since there are so many attractive ties with clan badges or society arms on them. Some object to a striped tie with the kilt, but to me a school or regimental tie does not look out of place. In this whole area, obviously, the authorities disagree, so you might as well please yourself.

Military shirts open up a whole new subject, because they are an item of uniform. This means that they are perfectly all right for pipe bands, because pipe bands wear uniforms—each band a uniform of its own. This is particularly true of headgear. You will see every possible form of Scottish bonnet and even British colonial *topis* and Arab *kaffiyehs*.

The problem arises because a short-sleeved uniform shirt is a very practical summer garment with the kilt. So you will see them worn, not only plain, but with tartan shoulder tabs and even pocket flaps. You will also see them worn with military ribbon bars, and this brings you up against my contention that the kilt is not a uniform, except in a pipe band. The Scottish-American Military Society disagrees with me, at least to the extent that they approve wearing a military shirt, complete with ribbons, qualification badges, and patches, but not insignia of rank or branch of service, with the kilt. I don't specially like this, but if I tried to tell S.A.M.S. it was wrong, they'd tell me to go whistle up a rope.

BUT, if you're going to wear a military shirt, let it conform to military regulations! No tartan, nothing you wouldn't wear with uniform. And DON'T wear ribbons with a non-military jacket. Don't mix civilian and military attire! Except miniature medals with evening wear; you'd wear them with Saxon evening wear, too.

There is no regulation covering the carrying of tartan banners in the Parade of Tartans, but it would make sense to adopt the rules that apply to the regimental color: keep your bonnet on; you're "under arms," and the banner could be dipped—just like the regimental color—during national anthems and "The Flowers of the Forest."

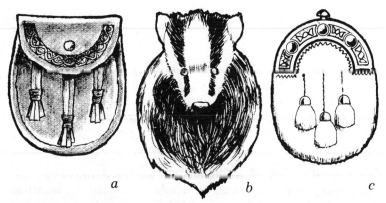

Figure 11. a) Plain leather for day wear. b) Animal mask which has the unique advantage of being correct for all occasions. c) Silver mounted fur for evening wear.

SPORRANS

With the kilt, a sporran is a real necessity. You have to have some place to put whatever you usually carry in your pants pockets. The only sporran that will serve for all occasions is the fur sporran with the animal's head made into the flap that closes it. These animal-mask sporrans are very expensive (all but the plainest leather sporrans are) and hard to get, since badgers and otters are now protected, though I understand the sporran makers are importing badger skins from Texas. Someone should get into the business over here. A marmot is just the right size for a sporran, and the eastern marmot, *marmota virginiana,* is the woodchuck, a farm pest that is not likely ever to get on anybody's protected list. In the first edition of this book I suggested that a skunk-skin sporran, with its black and white, would look well with the black and silver of Scottish evening dress. A taxidermist in Nova Scotia took up this suggestion, and skunk-skin, animal-mask sporrans are now available. Sporrans of all styles are shown in figure 11.

You have two options, unless expense is no object. The first is to get a plain leather sporran to wear with your kilt jacket and start saving up for an evening sporran. Your evening outfit is going to run into money, anyway. The other alternative is to buy a not-too-fancy evening sporran and wear it for both day and evening. This is not too good. For evening wear, the sporran must be fur and silver mounted. This is not going to look well with a sports jacket or even more informal outfits. And the purists who talk of "hunting attire" will boggle at the glittering silver. You are going to want two sporrans in the end, and one of them should be plain leather, so the best deal in the long run is to get that one first. If you can do simple leather work, the appendix (p. 112) gives patterns for simple day sporrans.

They are now manufacturing sporrans with fur fronts and leather around the edges. These appear to me to be neither flesh, fowl, nor good red herring. They definitely are not dressy enough for evening, and that being so, there is no warrant for spending the extra that they cost over a plain leather sporran.

If you have a chance to shop for a sporran (rather than mail ordering) be sure it is roomy. You will have to carry in it a money clip for bills and credit cards, a coin purse (loose coins in a sporran are hopeless), and your driver's license and car keys, at very least. So try to find a sporran with a mouth you can get your hand into. An old and most convenient pattern of soft leather with drawstrings is now being revived. (See Appendix, p. 112 and fig. 7b.)

Don't wear the sporran too low! The top of a small sporran should not be lower than about a hand's breadth below your navel. If you wear a hair sporran—and it is not recommended except for bandsmen—the top must be even higher, because the bottom should not come down below the bottom of the kilt. One of my advisers in Scotland says that no sporran should be worn more than a couple of inches below the navel. He points out quite correctly that this height is far more comfortable, particularly when you are really active as when running or dancing. If you decide to wear your sporran so, however, you must put up with the fact that you will be wearing it a few inches higher than other people. There is nothing, of course, to prevent you from adjusting the height to the occasion. Wear the sporran at the stylish height until you are about to start running or dancing, and then take up the strap a couple of holes! For really violent activities like tossing the caber or throwing the hammer, the sporran is, of course, laid aside completely.

Some kilts have little belt loops in back to put the sporran straps through, but I have found them useless and inconvenient. A sporran on a strap or chain of the right length hangs perfectly well without any further support. And in ballroom dancing the sporran must be put out of the way by sliding it over onto the left hip. If the strap or chain is confined in back, this becomes a real hassle. Except for evening, use a strap on your sporran, rather than a chain! The chain chafes the kilt and wears it out much faster than a strap.

PLAIDS

Plaids are confusing, but only because of the terminology. To keep this straight, let's take them one at a time. The first is the piper's plaid, though its use, as we shall see, is not confined to bandsmen. This is simply a piece of tartan, double width (52 to 56 inches) and three and a half yards long. It is fringed at both ends. It is worn with civilian day dress when a person wants to wear tartan above the waist. It can also be used as a lap rug. It is not worn pinned over the shoulder as a piper wears it. The plaid is first folded lengthways to bring the two selvages together. A second lengthways fold brings the first fold to the selvages, and the plaid is now full length but only a quarter its normal width. It is finally folded in half to bring the two fringed edges together. The final result is laid over the shoulder with the fringed ends hanging in front. Figure 13a shows a man in day dress with this shoulder plaid.

The second plaid we need to discuss is the belted plaid or *breacan feile*. This is pronounced "breck'n failer" with the final "r" dropped in Saxon fashion. It means "kilted tartan" in Gaelic. This also was a piece of double width tartan, but 4½ to 6 yards long. The wearer put his belt down on the ground, or on a bed if a bed was handy, and pleated the *breacan*—which he had slept rolled up in— over it lengthways, as shown in figure 12a. Some 16" was left unpleated at each end, and the rest of the five yards or so was kilted over the belt so that the whole back was pleats and the length was reduced to just enough to go round the wearer's waist with the unpleated ends overlapping in front.

This was just one way of doing it. Some of the old pictures of the *breacan feile* show pleats all the way round

Figure 12. Putting on the breacan feile. *a) It is first folded over the wearer's belt on the ground or on a bed if one is handy. b)The wearer lies down and belts it on, smoothing the two aprons at the ends over each other. c) When he stands up the inside layer (invisible) is just like a kilt: two crossed aprons in front and pleats all around the back. The outside layer hangs down to mid-calf like a sort of maxi-kilt. There are many possible arrangements for this outside layer, one shown in figure 9b.*

the front. Also the process we are in the middle of describing would hardly have been followed by a garrison or encampment in case of a surprise night attack. As a matter of fact, we don't really know for sure how the *breacan* was put on. Nobody wrote a description, because everybody knew how it was done, having learned as a boy. Imagine a historian of a couple of centuries from now trying to find a written description of how to tie your shoelaces or pin a safety pin! Nobody writes these instructions down, because everybody has learned how to do these things before he knows how to read.

But let's go back to our victim, who was left standing in his shirttails with his *breacan feile* kilted over his belt on the bed or on the ground. He now lies down with his waist over the belt, and buckles the belt on, smoothing the two unfolded "aprons" over each other in front (see fig. 12b). When he stands up, the *breacon feile* hangs down around him on all sides. The part under his belt is just like a kilt, except that the pleats are not pressed or sewn in. There are the same two aprons crossing in front, with the sides and back pleated all the way round. The outer part hangs down to mid-calf like a sort of maxi-kilt (see fig. 12c).

There are many things he can do now. If he is just slouching around camp, he may let it hang. To get more completely dressed, he puts on jacket, belt, and sporran, rolls up the right side of the top of the *breacan,* and tucks it into his belt. The left side may be draped over his left arm, or it may be brought up to his left shoulder and secured with a brooch. In bad weather, the top part is pulled up over both shoulders like a cape to protect the wearer from the rain.

This was the trouble with the *breacan feile,* of course, and the reason why it was developed into the kilt. When a man came in out of the weather with the top part of his plaid soaking, there was no way he could take it off to dry without undressing. If he could have detached the top part of the *breacan,* the bottom part would have promptly slipped out from under his belt, and he would be no better off. The only way the top could be made detachable would be to sew the pleats into the bottom half part way down from the waist. As soon as you did this you had a kilt. When, where, and by whom this was first done is one of the hottest arguments in the whole history of Scottish attire—an argument that I am happy to stay out of. The kilt was known as the "philabeg," the same root as our *feile* that means "kilted," and *beg* for "small." The spelling with "ph" was a product of the Classical Revival, where any possible new word was spelled with the Greek "phi." Then the word "philamore" was backformed (*mor* means "big") to refer to the *breacan feile.*

It would be nice—I'm giving my opinion free rein again—if more people wore the *breacan feile.* It is not quite as convenient as a kilt, though this can be partly overcome by sewing on belt loops. Nor is that cheating; the old texts mention a man putting on his *breacan feile,* which his gillie holds with the belt through the keepers. You need one loop for each pleat of the kilt part, and if you make them the full width of the pleat, simply stringing them onto a belt leaves the *breacan feile* ready to wear. The *breacan feile* has two real advantages: it makes a splendid full-dress outfit with one of the better doublets and lace jabot (see fig. 9b) and it saves the expense of getting kilt after kilt for a growing boy. Furthermore it is available for the cost of the yard goods.

The third and last type of plaid is worn with evening dress. It is supposed to make the wearer look somewhat as though he were wearing a *breacan feile,* even though it is just an accessory to the usual kilt. It is often called a "belted plaid," but this is confusing, since that term is also used for the *breacan feile.* That is why we used the Gaelic for *breacan feile,* and to continue to avoid the confusion, we will call the present garment an "evening plaid." Calling it an evening plaid also points up the fact that it should not be worn with day wear.

This is one of the commonest mistakes made by American wearers of Scottish attire. One sees pictures of Americans at Highland Games accompanying visiting chiefs from Scotland. If the Scot has any tartan above the waist, it is the folded plaid laid over the shoulder.

The American will have an evening plaid fastened at the shoulder by a "poached-egg" brooch. The contrast is appalling. This time I am not expressing just a personal opinion. If anyone cares to confirm it, I suggest that he write to someone in Scotland who habitually wears the kilt. In my personal opinion (which anyone is free to disagree with) the evening plaid is even too dressy to go well with the Prince Charlie coatee. As I have said (and will say later at least once more—sorry!), I like to see the Prince Charlie kept as simple as possible, saving the plaid, jabot, and dirk for full dress.

The evening plaid is a rectangle of tartan, pleated at one end, that attaches to the waist with a belt or tape. The other three sides are fringed like the ends of a piper's plaid, and there is a knot of fringe midway of the end opposite the pleated end. This knot goes under the shoulder-strap of the doublet and fastens with a brooch. We have said that the evening plaid and kilt together are supposed to give the effect of the *breacan feile*. This in spite of the fact that the original *breacan feile* probably did not have a fringe. The MacIan drawing that shows the back view of the *breacan feile,* however, shows it with a deep fringe, and this may well have been the source for those who invented the evening plaid in Victorian times. They were much less critical of MacIan's historical accuracy then than we are now. Some who wear the *breacan feile* for full-dress evening attire put a fringe around the whole top half, and a knot of fringe to fasten to the shoulder. This is a clear backformation, with the original imitating the imitation, and the purists take a predictably dim view of it. However, it is dressy and differs less from the standard evening plaid. An evening plaid is shown in figure 8b, and directions for making your own are in the appendix (p. 116).

IN COLD WEATHER

Firstly, don't be afraid to wear your kilt in the cold! You will have good, warm socks inside stout shoes, and your exposed knees are all skin and bone, and don't feel the cold at all keenly. The kilt itself is many thicknesses of wool, so all you need to concern yourself with is the upper part of your body. Again you should suit the formality of your dress to the occasion. If you are hiking, the usual sweaters and hooded jackets are the thing to wear.

For more formal wear the answer is not so simple. The correct overcoat, of course, is an Inverness cape (see fig. 13b), and you should get one as soon as you can get it into your budget. I suppose I should apologize here to any of my readers who do not have budget problems. If you can sink hundreds of dollars into your Scottish outfit without turning a hair, then of course get an Inverness cape, and a dark cape for evening wear. My remarks on jackets and sporrans will have been superfluous, too, for anyone who will buy two of each right at the beginning. For those of us who do have to live on a budget, the dark cape may prove easier than the Inverness. The Navy boat cloak and the similar capes used for full dress by other services do very well with formal Scottish attire, day or evening. You may be able to find one of these at a service thrift shop or even a surplus store.

Figure 13. Accessories. a) The long walking stick is the cromach. A piper's plaid is folded and carried over the shoulder. The long laced gillie shoes are detailed in the insert. b) The Inverness cape is the correct overgarment with the kilt.

If you have to wear a Saxon overcoat with the kilt, the best choice is a fabric raincoat that hangs as much like a cape as possible. A trench coat is not bad if you do not buckle it. As a matter of fact, any coat should be left unbuttoned if the weather permits, to show the sporran and the front of the kilt. To me a Saxon overcoat looks better if it is not longer than the kilt itself, though the Inverness cape is of course longer.

FOOTWEAR

The purists insist on polished black shoes with the kilt, but this is probably a hang-over from service regulations. There is nothing dreadfully wrong with brown shoes or even suede. Keep the shoes at the proper level of formality with the rest of your outfit! For usual day wear this will mean polished leather, and for evening, patent leather with silver buckles. On very informal occasions, such as picnics or other outings, hiking shoes or suede shoes are perfectly acceptable. In very hot weather, I have even worn brown canvas slip-on shoes, and no one minded. Very few people look at your feet, and unless you are wearing something pretty startling, you will do all right.

You can get patent leather evening shoes with silver buckles in several styles, and anything that a good outfitter offers as a Scottish evening shoe is likely to be perfectly correct. The commonest styles are a slip-on that comes a bit futher over the instep than a Saxon evening shoe, and another slipper style that has a strap over the instep. This "Mary Jane" looks a bit odd to an American—like Alice in Wonderland from the Tenniel illustrations—but it is a perfectly standard Scottish evening style for men (see fig. 8b). Any plain, black, patent-leather, slip-on shoe will do, as long as you can figure a way to attach the buckles. With the Prince Charlie, you can even get by without evening shoes. Any well polished black shoes, such as you might wear with a tuxedo, will serve.

There is a specially Scottish style of shoe that comes in versions for day, evening, and country dancing. These are known as gillie shoes, and have long laces crossing back and forth over the open instep and then tying around the ankle (see fig. 13a). They are in black leather for day, black patent leather for evening, and soft soled for dancing. Gillie shoes add a very nice touch, but except for the dancing shoes, they are rather expensive, even as good shoes go. For any kind of day wear, gillie shoes are optional. You are always correct in any style of polished leather shoes. For the more formal styles of day wear, these should be black for preference.

Stockings can be a problem, since good kilt hose are hard to get at the present writing, and very expensive. Also the ones that have been available shrink dreadfully at the slightest provocation. So if you lay out the necessary sum for a pair of tartan evening hose, be sure that they are carefully hand washed in cool water with dry-cleaning powder or the mildest of soaps. Remember, too, that tartan hose are for evening only! They are not correct for day wear. On that basis, a good pair should last you a lifetime. Diced hose in blue and white or red and white have always been an alternative choice for evening wear, and since even these are hard to come by, you will see many men in evening attire with solid color stockings. The purists have given in on this point, but they insist that the only correct color is white.

You will have two problems with regular kilt hose. One is expense, even of the plain ones for day wear, and the other is that they are heavy wool. This is fine in Scotland, but at some of the games in the South at the height of the summer, wool socks get awfully hot. You may be able to solve the price problem by shopping around the skiers' and hikers' stores. I found some good Norwegian wool socks at about a third the going price for kilt hose. They don't shrink too badly, either, but they are even heavier than the usual Scottish product.

You may be able to find lighter weight socks in a regular men's store. Many good grades of over-the-calf men's socks in the stretch varieties will come up far enough to turn down over the garters. Kilt hose should not be too long in any case. As long as they come up high enough over the calf for the garters to hold, that is plenty. They should never cover any part of the bony structure of the knees. Careful shopping should turn up socks in reasonable weights and colors. Dark hose are desirable in any case with the more formal dark day jackets. And don't neglect the ladies' stores! I have found excellent "walking socks" for young misses that, in the stretch styles, were fine for wear with the kilt. The larger sizes, intended for the plumper lasses stretch equally well vertically to come up a longer leg.

The simplest kind of garters are the plain elastic ones fastening with a metal hook arrangement. If your Scottish supply store is out of stock, the same thing is an item of Boy Scout uniform. Once in a pinch away from home when I found I hadn't packed my garters, I got a pair at a store that sold supplies for Brownie Girl Scouts. There should be garter flashes that hang down below the turned down tops of the hose. These are generally red or green, to go with the predominant color of the kilt. For evening wear they should be silk and may be of tartan silk if you can find them. For day wear they are of wool or braid. The flashes should come forward of the side of the leg. The middle of the back one should not be further back than the middle of the side of the leg, and no part of the front one should be past the center of the front of the leg. This gives you a good bit of latitude except on a pair of real spindle shanks.

There is also a wrap-around garter, made of wool or the same braid as the garter flashes, and having its own flashes sewn to it at right angles. This goes twice around the leg, and the end tucks in. The last bit should be folded at forty-five degrees, to give a tab that tucks neatly behind the horizontal folds. This may be sewn in as described in the appendix (see p. 119). The wrap-around garter is less lumpy under the turned down hose tops and is also more comfortable. When carefully wrapped it will even hold up a skene dhu through the most vigorous dance.

Neither of these styles, particularly the first, can properly be worn with castellated hose, which do not turn down over the garter (see fig. 9b). For a long time you never saw castellated hose except in fashion drawings, but on his last trip to Scotland my good friend Jim Monroe, Past President of the Saint Andrew's Society of Washington, DC, persuaded Jonathan Ross of Inverness to start making them again. The real original garters were a woven or knitted tube, and if you can find a fabric store with a really complete line of trimmings, you can still get this. It is called knitted fold-over braid, and you will need a couple of yards for each garter. The appendix (p. 119) tells how to tie the knot, which is a bit complicated, but not really difficult after you get a little practice. You may not need the full two yards for each garter, but after you have practiced tying the knot a couple of times you can cut them to length. If you can't get this fold-over braid, don't worry. Some of the older pictures show a much narrower garter, and I recently saw a pair of castellated hose held up with what looked like the heavy wool hair ties that you can get at any notions counter. It looked very much like what you see in some of the old paintings. The hair ties can also be tied in the old knot if they are long enough. I have also seen castellated hose with the usual wrap-around garter. I didn't like this as well, but it wasn't really bad.

Added for the second edition: the shoes-must-be-black question has finally been settled definitively. Scottish shoemakers are now making gillie shoes—which cost a young fortune—in brown as well as black, and I can't imagine anyone wearing gillies except with the kilt. Of course the really dedicated purists will still say they're wrong.

DIRKS AND SKENE DHUS

I am often called down for writing "skene dhu" instead ot *sgian dubh*. My answer is that I am writing English, and you will find "skene dhu" in any good English dictionary. I am not against using a Gaelic word when it is called for, as witness *breacan feile*, used above to avoid confusion. But I see no more reason for writing *sgian dubh* than for writing *mukesin* for "moccasin" or *juzgado* for "hoosegow." I admit I am an extremist on this point; I even prefer "cream of mint" to *crème de menthe*, unless I am talking to a Frenchman.

But to start with dirks: the dirk is an item of evening wear. It should be black handled and the sheath should be black morocco or patent leather. Silver mounting is desirable, and jewels may be added. In fact, the whole thing except the blade may be of jewelled silver. It usually has a miniature knife and fork in smaller sheaths on the side of the big sheath. These are frequently attached by little chains, to be sure that they will be absolutely useless. If I ever get a dirk, it will not have them. a typical dirk is shown in figure 14.

I don't like to see a dirk with a Prince Charlie coatee, though it would be putting it too strongly to say that this is incorrect. But I will say (I hope for the last time) that I like to see the Prince Charlie kept as simple as possible, with black tie and black shoes and no ornaments past the plain evening belt, and shoe buckles if you choose. And a dirk is not for day wear unless you choose to go armed. Even in this case it should not be jewelled or silver mounted. A Scottish friend assures me that he carries a dirk when hill walking and finds many uses for it. I am reminded of the time I was reproved by

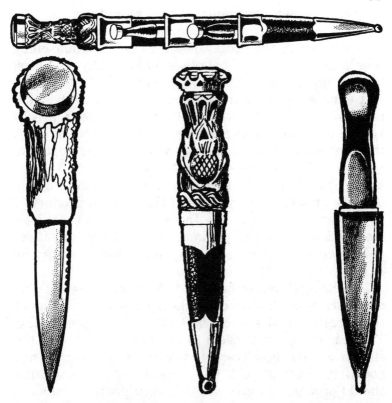

Figure 14. Dirk and skene dhus. The dirk (top) is an evening style and the center skene dhu matches it. The plain handle at right may be of horn or plastic and the handle at left is made from the base of a stag's antler.

an experienced outdoorsman for carrying a sheath knife. He assured me there was nothing I could do with it that I could not do better with a pocket knife or a small axe, except skin a large animal. Even this exception does not apply to a dirk; it would make a lousy skinning knife.

The skene dhu, by contrast, is not a weapon; it is a utility knife. I read recently that someone in Scottish attire was refused entry to the House of Commons until he removed his skene dhu. He should have held out, because the short skene dhu was adopted during the proscription when weapons were forbidden to the Highlanders. The House of Commons has enough opportunity to heckle the Scots when they refuse a man entry if he is carrying a set of bagpipes. They are, by definition of an English court, a weapon of war.

It is hard to find a good skene dhu. Most of them are made of stainless steel that will not hold an edge, even if you take the trouble to give them one. So we will discuss them merely as ornament. And by the way as an optional ornament. You are perfectly properly dressed without a skene dhu. Personally I would rather do without one in the day time than carry some of the feckless products I have seen offered for sale. In evening dress the silver-mounted jewel at the pommel of the skene dhu looks quite nice peeping out of the top of the hose (see figs. 9a & 14).

This brings up another point. You often see a skene dhu worn with the top of the hose even with the top of the sheath and the whole haft of the knife protruding. The reasoning would seem to be that if you use it, the sheath will be right there so you can put it back. This, however, is not correct. Only enough of the skene dhu should protrude to give you a firm grip when you want it. When you put it back, you either dig the sheath out of your sock or pull the top of your sock open far enough to find the sheath so you can replace the knife.

The skene dhu goes in your sock because it is too long to go into the sporran. Anything else that fits this description may also be carried in the sock, including a tobacco pipe or reading glasses. And if you are left handed, there is nothing wrong with wearing the skene dhu on the left leg.

The jewelled skene dhu may also be worn with day wear, though the purists frown on the silver and jewel with their "hunting" attire. I have never seen a jewelled skene dhu that was a usable knife, so you might as well humor them by going without. Unless, of course, you want to get a day skene dhu. These are available with a plain horn or plastic handle, or with a handle made from the base of a deer's antler. The latter is very handsome, and if you can find a plastic handle on a decent piece of steel, you will have a usable knife (see fig. 14). If I bear down on the utility of the skene dhu, it is because I have carried a sharp pocket knife for half a century and like to have an equally useful skene dhu. At our society luncheons one of the members likes to sit next to me so he can borrow my skene dhu to cut his post-prandial cigar.

The blades of most skene dhus have, like the dirk, longitudinal blood grooves and nicked backs which are supposed to be fish scalers. This is a bit silly. The dirk is a stabbing weapon, so blood grooves are functional, but they are quite out of place on a utility knife. And anyone who knows how to scale a fish knows that the implement to use is a teaspoon.

THE CROMACH

This is the crook-handled walking stick that is particularly suited to use with Scottish attire. The British are much more used to walking sticks than the Americans. When you visit a large house and the host is going to take you out to show you over his grounds, he will often offer you a walking stick to use. The Saxons are partial to a crook-handled cane that comes to the height of your hand as it hangs at your side. The cromach is longer, how much longer is a matter of individual taste and considerable discussion. Your hands folded on top of the crook should come somewhere at chest height, but this can be anywhere from just above the solar plexus to the collar-bone (see fig. 13a).

The crook of the cromach may be of wood integral with the staff. For this the maker must find a clump of hazel and take one of the outer stems, digging it out root and all. The root will have the proper curve and the stem will be straight. A commoner form of cromach has the handle of horn, joined to the wooden staff by a silver band. In either case, the end of the handle usually curves back to form a ball which is surmounted by a carved thistle.

WEAPONS

At the height of the Victorian period, the way to win the "best dressed Highlander" award was to hang on to all the weapons you could think of. This included broadswords, pistols, and powder horns.

Swords—whether broadswords or claymores—Lochaber axes, and similar cutlery are weapons and have no place in civilian Scottish attire. A drum major may carry a broadsword, but he is in uniform. You may also see weapons and targes in the procession that escorts the haggis in, but none of these could be considered part of normal civilian dress. Dirks are weapons, too, but we have already discussed them (see p. 88). Scottish flintlock pistols and powder horns are available, usually in highly decorated forms. The powder horns have often been converted to whisky flasks. You will see them worn with evening dress, but they are definitely out of place except with full dress (doublets and lace). Even then they are in doubtful taste, but that last is a personal opinion—possibly influenced by the fact I've never been able to afford either!

JEWELRY

The first item to mention is the kilt pin, and the first thing to say is that it is optional. Even if you wear one, don't pin it though anything but the top apron! It would ruin the hang of the kilt, and you would have to pin and unpin it every time you dressed. When Queen Victoria modestly ruled that all military kilts should have a means of fasteninng the outer apron to the inner, some regiments selected the kilt pin. The Black Watch, however, used ribbons, which remain in the green-ribbon decoration in the kilt-pin position. Neither method was actually used functionally. The soldiers were much too proud of the hang of their kilts.

Some people base a dislike for kilt pins on this history. An added disadvantage is that a kilt pin may snag on something and leave you a nasty tear in the exposed apron of your kilt. If you want to take this chance, the danger may be minimized by buttonhole-stitching two tiny holes for the pin to go through.

If you wear a kilt pin, you may like to match the kilt pin to the formality of your dress, using a plain blanket pin for sport dress, something more ornate for more formal day wear, and jewelled silver for evening. In the design of the kilt pin, you can choose one of the traditional patterns, or you can let your imagination run riot. Just don't let it get too big and heavy or it will drag down that side of the kilt!

Other jewelry for day wear is limited to cufflinks and tie-clips or tie-tacks. These can get fancier as your dress gets more formal. A lapel pin of your society arms can often be converted into a tie-tack, which is suitable for any wear. With more formal day wear jewelled cufflinks look well. The traditional stones for Scottish jewelry are cairngorm and amethyst. The former is a rock crystal that comes in colors from yellow-orange to smoky grey.

You may be able to buy cufflinks and tie-clips with the arms of your chief on them, but it is entirely improper for you to wear them. Arms are the personal property of one man, and using another man's arms in Scotland is a punishable offense. I have heard that some chiefs have granted their clansmen permission to wear jewelry with their arms, but this still does not make it correct. The most the chief can possibly do is promise not to prosecute his clansmen for what remains an infringement of his right to the sole use of the arms. Even this would not protect his clansmen in Scotland from prosecution by the Procurator Fiscal to the Lyon Court.

Evening jewelry, in addition to cufflinks and shirt studs (if you wear a shirt that takes studs), may include a silver belt buckle, plaid brooch, and a pin for the jabot. All of these may carry one or more stones, either cairngorm or amethyst. It is preferable to have the same kind of stone in all your jewelry and accessories, though it may be a bit difficult to find a dirk and skene dhu set with amethyst. These nearly always come with a cairngorm. Most of us, of course, settle for paste imitations rather than real gems, either of cairngorm or amethyst.

MEDALS AND DECORATIONS

It is always correct to wear medals and decorations with Scottish evening wear, though it is not necessary unless the invitation specifies them. Since the kilt is not a uniform, medals are worn on the left side of the jacket, not on the lapel. If there is a breast pocket, the medals should be just above it. If there is no pocket, the medals go just above where a pocket would be. For evening wear the medals should be miniatures, and miniatures should never be worn with anything but evening dress.

Medals are also properly worn with civilian clothing in a parade. This does not arise on many occasions except in Scottish attire. But overseas Scots are great on parades, including a peculiarly American church parade, universally known as the "Kirkin' o' the Tartan." In a parade you will not be wearing evening dress, so the medals should not be miniatures. It may feel a bit odd wearing the large "gongs" when you are not in uniform, but for parades it is the proper thing.

The rules of the Scottish-American Military Association on wearing medal ribbons on military shirts with the kilt appear under "Shirts and Ties" (see p. 73). Note that *nobody* sanctions wearing ribbon bars on anything but uniform. NEVER wear them on a kilt jacket. Miniature medals? Yes—with evening wear, just as with Saxon evening wear. Full-sized gongs? Yes—in parades (see above). Ribbon bars? NEVER—except as prescribed by S.A.M.S. (see p. 73). I hope that makes it clear enough!

It is just as wrong to make a uniform out of Scottish attire as it is to make a costume out of it.

THE FINAL QUESTION

This is, of course: what do you wear under the kilt? I hope I will be forgiven for quoting the old, tired, but classic responses: "Nothing worn, Madam; everything in first-class working order." and "I'm a man o' few words, Madam; gi'e me your hand!" In this family of jokes, the inquirer is always a lady, usually an old maid. But joking aside, this is a question that needs to be answered.

There is one firm answer—in Army uniform regulations, though I am told that these differ in detail from one regiment to another. A highland soldier in the kilt is out of uniform if he wears anything under it except when dancing, taking part in Highland games, or participating as a bandsman. If that last exception puzzles you, watch the way a band marks time with the knees coming up to waist height.

The civilian may please himself. If you are dancing or throwing the hammer, or if you just decide to wear pants anyway, you might try something that you would not consider wearing under trousers. I mean the men's "bikini" shorts. These can be slipped off in case of an urgent call of nature without unduly disarranging the kilt. The same cannot be said of underpants that come up to normal waist height.

For normal wearing of the kilt, many men prefer the military practice. In fact I may say that I never knew of a man who gave it a fair trial that ever went back to wearing pants under the kilt. In the old days with the *breacan feile,* of course, underclothes were unheard of. But they wore their shirts long enough to knot the tails between their legs when they went into battle without their plaids. If you have your shirts tailor made, you might want to get some with at least the back tail long enough so that you are sitting on linen. Without going to that extent, you can go to a store that caters to large and tall men and get some extra length undershirts. Compare the different brands before you buy! Some are substantially longer than others. With or without these expedients, you will still find the military style far more comfortable.

Whatever the facts may be, you must never admit you are wearing pants under the kilt. This is part of the mystique. And when you say you are not, peole are usually incredulous. A friend of mine, on meeting with this incredulity, always says, "You are welcome to check," adding if it is a man, "if you think you are man enough." He says he has never met a man who thought he was man enough or a lady who was not too much of a lady. Another friend, however, says, "He never travelled with the girls in our crowd." Still I borrowed the gag and used it myself on a TV interview in New York—with a man interviewer, I should add.

SOME FINAL CAUTIONS

I hate to end on a negative note, but there are a few mistakes that are made so often that they should be mentioned again:

DON'T get your kilt too long! The top of the knee is the absolute long limit, and up to an inch shorter is acceptable—better in my personal opinion.

DON'T pin a kilt pin through both aprons of your kilt! It will spoil the hang of the kilt and be a bother getting it on and off.

DON'T wear a Balmoral bonnet with the ribbons trailing behind! The ribbons of any bonnet should be at the center of the back, and our illustrations show the proper angle for each.

DON'T wear eagle feathers (or a substitute) in your bonnet because you are "chief" or "chieftain" of an American society! The use of feathers is best limited to those whose right to wear them has been established by the Lord Lyon.

DON'T mix day wear and evening wear! Tartan hose, jewelled dirk, miniature medals, and evening plaid are not proper for daytime wear. These may look dressy to you, but they make you look stupid to anyone—in particular a visiting Scot—who knows how to wear the kilt.

If you have only one sporran, you will have to wear it with everything, but a silver-mounted fur sporran does not look well with informal day wear, and a plain leather sporran looks even worse with evening wear. The animal-mask sporran has the advantage of going with anything.

So for a final up-beat:

DO wear the kilt early and often! You'll find that everyone likes to see you in the kilt. You'll be amazed at the lack of negative reaction, and indeed at the lack of any reaction whatever. I have worn the kilt into bars, restaurants, service stations, stores, and other public places, and 99% of the time no notice is taken of my attire. The odd occasion has varied from a joyous greeting in the Canadian Embassy, "It's been *so* long since we've seen a man in a kilt," to the opening of a pleasant conversation about things Scottish.

APPENDIX

This appendix will tell you things you can do or make to improve your Scottish attire, or to get the necessary items at a price less than what you pay on the open market. Scottish attire is unfortunately very expensive, but there are several ways to get around this. If you know a really good seamstress, and can borrow a good kilt to go by, even a kilt is not beyond the limits of possibility. No kiltmaker will admit this, and there are secrets to kiltmaking that the kiltmakers boast of. None of them are vital nor beyond discovery if a good seamstress examines a kilt. I will grant that a professional kiltmaker can undoubtedly spot a homemade kilt and even tell a well made professional kilt from a run-of-the-mill job, but very few of the people who see you in the kilt will be professional kiltmakers. And the vast majority of the rest of your outfit can be improvised or modified, as described below.

I hope this appendix will not make me too many enemies in the tartan trade. Actually I feel that I am doing them a good turn. If a young man gets into the habit of wearing Scottish attire before he can afford the full outfit, he is likely to continue and want to get the professionally made articles later on when he is better off financially.

THE BALMORAL BONNET

The only alternative to buying a bonnet is to go bareheaded, and if you choose the Glengarry the only modification that would apply is the change of the cockade. But the Balmoral needs to have some work done on the ribbons. Some Balmorals are coming through these days with the ribbons already knotted. All you need to do with these is to untie the knot, press the ribbons and retie them, trimming the ends to length if necessary, as it usually will be after retying the knot. Then take a stitch or two through the knot to keep it tied!

If the ribbons are not tied, the simplest thing, as we have said, is just to cut them off, but this is really cheating. We will bet, though, that no one who has not read this book will notice if you do. But let's do it right! You will find that the ribbons are sewn to each other for the first couple of inches. The stitches must be picked out, taking care not to cut the ribbons. Then tie a bow knot 3" to 3½" across the bows! This will leave a considerable long end of each ribbon, which must be cut off on the bias, the point extending just a little past the end of the bow. Then a stitch or two through the knot will keep it tied.

A dark Balmoral may also have a red toorie, which may look better if you replace it with a dark one. The red toorie on a Glengarry should not be changed; that is the right color. Of course the red toorie on the Balmoral is perfectly correct, too, but if you want to replace it, this is how to go about it. First off, you have to match the color, and this may not be easy. Most dark Balmorals are not black and they are darker blue than most wool you

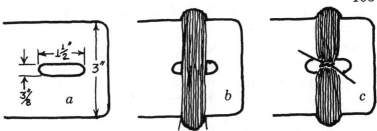

Figure 15. Tying a toorie. a) The card you need. b) The wool wound on. c) Tying the knot.

can find. The solution is to use the nearest color, either black or dark blue, or to mix the colors. It will take very careful inspection to tell the difference. You will need a card, cut as shown out of a corrugated cardboard carton. The wool, black, blue, or a strand of each is wound round the card until the hank is about ¾" wide and ½" deep as shown. Then take some heavy thread—button and carpet thread will do, but waxed shoemaker's thread is better—and tie it around the whole hank, using the slit in the card to pass it around! The knot is pulled as tight as possible, but only the first half is tied at this time (see fig. 15). Now slip a sharp knife or the tip of a pair of scissors next to the card and cut the wool loose at both ends! The knot can now probably be pulled tighter and the second half of it tied. The resulting untidy bundle of wool is then trimmed down to a neat, round toorie, the size of the one you are replacing. A large needle now takes the ends of the thread separately through the middle of the bonnet, where they pass through the holes of a two-hole shirt button before being knotted and cut off. This completes the job.

Next to receive your attention is the cockade. There are only two reasons for changing this: to get rid of the Hanoverian black, or to use livery colors—those of the crest or badge that will be worn on it. If you are abolishing the Hanoverian black, you will want to replace it with Jacobite white, and a nice form for this is a Saint Andrew's cross. This should be of white grosgrain ribbon, not over 1¼" wide, and 1" is ample. Take two 7" pieces and cut the ends on the bias! If they are on the same bias, they will form a swallowtail when you fold the ribbon in the middle. Sew these in the place of the cockade you have removed! If you want to interlace them where they cross, this is nice, but not at all necessary. They don't need to be sewed down all round; just tacking the ends and a couple of times at the crossing will be plenty. There should be some place left to tuck a sprig of your plant badge behind the cockade. This is not done as often as it should be, but it is a very nice touch.

You should not wear a feather behind your cockade. Even if you have your own coat of arms and are entitled to a feather, the plain circlet—instead of a buckle and strap—bearing your motto is enough indication. It's nice to be a bit understated with this. Besides people seeing you with a feather are likely to group you with the "chiefs" and "chieftains" of Scottish societies who wear feathers because they don't know any better.

But to get back to cockades: the second reason for changing cockades is to get livery colors behind the crest or badge. The livery colors are almost always the first two colors named in the blazon of a coat of arms. If you are unfamiliar with the rules of blazon, that is not much help. But as you look at the shield, the two principal colors, one being gold (yellow) or silver (white), are most probably the ones. You can find most of the blazons in Adam (rev. Learney) *Clans, Septs, and Regiments of the Scottish Highlands.* The books don't say what to do if one of the colors is ermine. White fur with a black tail tip would look a bit out of place, so probably white would be the best answer. I have never heard of any arms where the principal colors are ermine and white, so at least this would get you off the hook.

Having chosen your colors, the next thing is to get the material for the cockade. This should be grosgrain ribbon, and the widest you can get. The cockade on your bonnet will probably have 3" ribbon, but 2½" or even 2¼" will do for the same kind of cockade you are taking off. A square of the white or yellow ribbon should be sewn in the position of the cockade, with the cut ends top and bottom. The proper space should be left for the stem

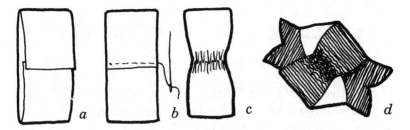

Figure 16. Making a two-color cockade. a) The folded rib-bon. b) The seam. c) The ribbon after gathering along the seam. d) The finished cockade.

of the plant badge. Next you need a piece about a third longer—4" if you are using 3" ribbon or 3" if you are us-ing 2¼". A needle threaded with the proper color now runs a fine in-and-out seem across the middle of this. The middle of the ribbon is gathered (puckered) along this seam and the seam finished off. This will give an hour-glass shape that is about square, which is sewed over the first square of ribbon with the cut ends front and back. This completes the cockade. Any time you are in doubt you can refer to the cockade you are removing. We do not even illustrate this one.

If you can only get narrow ribbon, ¾ inch or less, you will have to make a rosette. It should be of alternate loops of each color, starting at the bottom. You will have to use a little ingenuity when you get to the bottom again, and it will get rather thick in the middle and maybe messy, too, but the badge will cover this up. You should have about three inches of ribbon in each loop. The exact size is not critical, but they should be even.

The last kind of cockade is used with ribbon of inter-mediate width, say 1¼" to 1¾". This is illustrated step by step in fig. 16. First you need two bows, one in each color, made as follows. A piece of ribbon slightly more than 4 times as long as its width (6 1/8" of 1½" ribbon) is folded so that the ends overlap about 1/8" just at the middle of the ribbon. Then a fine seam is run through the three thicknesses—both ends and the middle of the rib-bon—and the seam is gathered and finished off, giving a slight hourglass shape. This is done again with the rib-

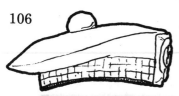

Figure 17. Shaping a Balmoral: before and after.

bon of the other color. Then a piece of the darker ribbon is cut, about an inch longer than the hourglass shapes, and its ends are cut in swallowtail shapes. This last piece is sewed to the bonnet first at an angle of about 20°, the front end higher. The hourglass of white or yellow ribbon comes next and finally that of darker ribbon, to give the result shown in the figure.

The final thing you may do to your Balmoral is suggested by the advice of Col. Ian Cameron-Taylor. This appeared in an article in "The SCOTS Magazine" and has been reprinted and distributed by the Scottish Tartans Society. His advice is that a bonnet is not ready to wear until it has lost all look of newness. To achieve this he recommends, as I recall, scuffing it ahead of your feet down a dusty path and then washing it in the nearest burn and wringing it out thoroughly. This leaves the fabric perfectly soft and limp, but it may have some deleterious effects on the binding and lining. You can get about the same effect with less wear and tear, though it may be considered cheating a bit. The right side of a new Balmoral sticks rather straight out like a shelf. When it is old and well worn, it droops down and lies against the side of the binding or the checkered portion of a checkered bonnet. So all you need to do is to sew it down to the binding, or about half way down the checkered portion. This is done by turning the bonnet inside out. With an uncheckered bonnet whipstitch the edge of the binding to the part of the bonnet that you want to have drooping to the right. This should come between your right ear and eyebrow. With a checkered bonnet sew them together, through and through about half way down the stiff checkered part or a bit lower. This will give the effect you want, with the slack of the bonnet on the right hanging down like a nice, old, comfortable bonnet, rather than sticking out stiffly.

TO SHORTEN A KILT

It is not easy to shorten a kilt, but it can be done, and it ought to be done far more often than it is. At any Highland gathering you will see not only kilts to mid-kneecap—which after all are just a bit old fashioned—but kilts that cover the whole knee, leaving just a sliver of white between them and the top of the hose. In cases like those something ought to be done, even at the risk of spoiling the kilt. It may be possible to cut off the top of a kilt, sew the pleats a bit further down, and bind the top as before, but I am not sure it would fit smoothly behind any more. Besides, there is an easier alternative.

Find someone with a clear eye and steady hand at the sewing machine, and have them run a seam at the level you want to cut the kilt off! This seam should be in strong, but not too heavy, thread. It must follow a single thread in the warp of the material all the way around the kilt. It is not critical if it runs a thread too high for a short space once or twice, but it should never catch the next lower thread. Then the kilt must be cut off just two threads lower than the seam. This again calls for a steady hand, a clear eye, and good light. It is not quite as critical to be exact here as when running the seam. The two threads below the seam are now unravelled all along.

The result is not quite the same as a kilt with a selvedge. If a dog grabbed you by the end of the kilt, it might pull loose with disastrous results. But it will stand up to any normal wear and tear, and it is far better than wearing a "trollopy" kilt. It is hard to express just how unpleasant a kilt looks when it is really too long.

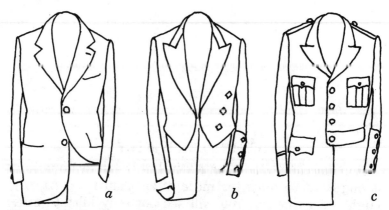

Figure 18. Jackets before and after. a) Suit jacket. b) Tail coat. c) Military blouse.

JACKETS

The only way out of the heavy expense of buying a kilt jacket is to have something retailored. Fortunately this is not too difficult. Figure 18 shows what you start with in the left half and what you end up with in the right. This makes it clearer than any other way of showing what you need to do. The suit coat can be almost any suit coat that the trousers have worn out on. Or you would be surprised at the nice suit coats you can pick up at Goodwill. The flashy suits and jackets are snapped up, and the conservative ones, which are what you want, are a drug on the market. The first really nice kilt jacket I ever had was tailored from an imported German jacket. I suspect it was tailor made; it is the only jacket I have ever seen where the cuff buttons actually unbutton, and I would be ashamed to tell you how little I paid for it.

The jacket must be shortened and cut away in front as shown in the illustration. The only problem with this is getting the cutaway shape right without hitting a buttonhole. If you start with a three-button suit, you should make a two-button kilt jacket, and with a two-button suit, end up with one button. Either is a perfectly satisfactory style. If you start the cutaway curve right at the last buttonhole you leave—and that is where the

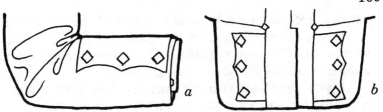

Figure 19. Prince Charlie coatee. a) Cuff. b) Tails.

cutaway should start, anyway—you should be able to miss the next buttonhole. The only other problem is pockets. If the jacket has patch pockets, they can be moved up bodily. Slit pockets present a bit of a problem. They are going to end up much too low, and there is no satisfactory way of raising them. You can, however, use the material you have cut off the bottom of the coat to make pocket flaps, and if properly placed, these will disguise the fact that the pockets are wrong (see fig. 18a).

You can't wear that jacket to the Tartan Ball; at some of them you would actually be turned away. So the next problem is an evening jacket, and it is easily solved. As we have said, you can pick up a tail coat at most tuxedo rental places, particularly after they have made their new year inventory. The tails must be cut off so that after the raw ends are hemmed they will come down just to the bottom of the stitched part of the kilt pleats. Then military cuffs must be added to the sleeves. These are shaped as shown and let into the upper seam of the sleeve. The sleeve cuff should be as long as it well may, without getting involved in the wrinkles when the man bends his arm. They may either be sewn down all round or fasten with snaps at the three points. The latter may be simplest and facilitates the attachment of the buttons, as there should be three silver buttons on each sleeve. This military cuff was where British officers, at least until World War I wore their insignia of rank: one to three pips for company officers and the crown sometimes with one or two pips for field officers. On the Prince Charlie coatee—which is the name of the jacket we are describing—everybody wears three square or diamond-shaped silver buttons (see fig. 19a). Each of the short coat tails has an attachment the same shape as the military cuff on the sleeve (see fig. 19b).

All you need now is more buttons. These are usually provided for—as are those on sleeve and coat tail—by a small, round buttonhole in the material. The button has a metal loop on the back that is put through this hole, and a fastener of one kind or another holds it in place. You need holes for two buttons—smaller ones—at the top of the coat tails, where the black buttons already are on the jacket as you get it. Then three buttons on each side of the front of the jacket. These are on a slight diagonal and can be spaced exactly as the three buttons on each sleeve (see fig. 18b).

A final jacket you may want to procure is the day doublet, and it is easily tailored from an Army, Air Force, or Marines uniform jacket, what the services call a "blouse." This jacket is intermediate in formality. With plastic buttons or buttons covered with the same material the doublet is made out of, and with a four-in-hand tie—the usual tie you wear with a business suit—it does very nicely for formal day wear. With silver buttons and black tie, it will get you by in the evening.

You start with the uniform jacket, either officer's or enlisted men's. This comes from the thrift shop at the nearest service installation. The first question is color. It will do very well in the color it comes in, but you might like to have it dyed. There are a couple of problems here: first where do you get it done? It used to be that every dry cleaner's had a dyer that worked with them, but it is not so easy to find a dyer these days. The next problem is shrinking. Almost no dyer will guarantee wool against shrinking when they dye it. You can take a chance, and if it shrinks pass the jacket along to a smaller man in your clan and start over with a larger jacket. If you are going to have it dyed, you have to do that first, anyway. If you do the tailoring first, the thread used may take a different color from the fabric.

Unless you are lucky enough to find one of the old tropical worsted blouses in the tan color, you are limited to a pretty dark final color, but that is all right. The day doublets I have seen range through all the shades: raspberry, aqua, and what have you, but a dark color will be fine.

Once it is dyed, or if you decide not to dye it, the rest is easy. You will want military cuffs as described for the Prince Charlie, but aside from that you simply cut it off at the waist and finish it with a waist band. This comes down over the top of your kilt, and you put a belt over it. The day doublet is a formal enough jacket so that it can take a black evening belt, even for day wear without a black tie (see fig. 18c).

We have mentioned that a Sheriffmuir doublet can be made from a Marine officer's mess dress uniform, but we are not going into details. This is a job for a professional tailor, and he will copy the cuffs and flaps from a piper's tunic.

SPORRANS

Plain leather sporrans are not unduly expensive, but those commercially available are next to useless. They are so small you can hardly get your hand into them, and you are likely to end up carrying practically everything in your jacket pockets. The problem is not overall size; the mouth of the sporran does not open wide enough to get into it. It is not difficult to make a leather sporran. You can cut the pieces and have them sewn by a shoemaker. If you do the advance work of putting the sporran together with rubber cement, the cost of running the seams should not be very great. Finding the leather may be a bit of a problem, but if you can find a Tandy Leather Co., they will have all you need. Of course if you are a skilled worker in the sort of thing the Tandy company caters to, you can make a very fancy sporran with carved leather and laced seams. You can get a design from George Bain's *Celtic Art—The Method of Construction*.

The illustrations show two styles of sporran. One of them looks very much like the usual leather sporran, but is made with a wider gusset, so you can get your hand into it. The other is a new style—actually a new revival of a very old style—and can be used on the usual sporran strap or on a waist belt. The latter practice was not at all unusual in the old days, and many people like it now. The first style illustrated (see fig. 20) should be made of heavy leather, 8- or 9-ounce steerhide. The front and back should be fastened together with a gusset—just a strip at least 1½ " wide—of the most flexible leather you can find that is strong enough to last. It need not match the front and back; a contrasting color could be attractive. The gusset should be cemented to the front and

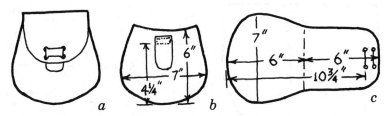

Figure 20. Conventional sporran. a) Finished view. b) Dimensions, front. c) Dimensions, back and flap.

back for 1/8" all round. You may need to wet and stretch the edges of the gusset where it goes around the curves so it will lie flat at the right angle. It must dry thoroughly again before being cemented. Then it must be sewed or laced together. The cover should then be folded down over the mouth and the folded part stood on end in a pan of water. When it is thoroughly soaked—and you might as well soak the whole sporran to avoid water staining—and dried again, the cover will remain in the closed position without a fastener. However you may use any fastener you choose. The figure shows a double slit in the cover and a strap sewed to the front of the sporran. If you use the dimensions shown, the strap will be just right for running through the two slits to hold the cover down. If you put the strap through the slits after you soak the sporran and let it dry there, it will be permanently molded into the proper shape to hold securely. Of course, the strap must be sewed to the front piece before the sporran is put together. Also before the sporran is put together, you should make arrangements for the carrying strap. You can cut pairs of double slits in the back or sew on little leather loops to pass the strap through. The latter is probably the best arrangement.

The second type of sporran is made of soft leather, the softer the better, so long as it is strong enough. Suede is fine. The back and front are cut to the size and shape shown in figure 21a. The cover flap is cut out of 8- or 9-ounce steerhide as shown and cemented to the middle of the outside of the back. Be sure that the middle of it,

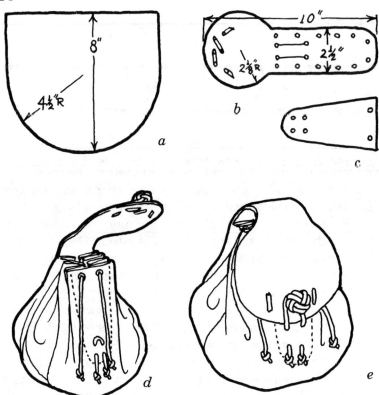

Figure 21. Pouch sporran. a) Front and back. b) Flap and back reinforcement. c) Front reinforcement. d) Finished sporran, partly closed. e) Fully closed.

under the belt loop, is not cemented! The holes around the edge must be an even number, so that a rawhide lace—a rawhide bootlace will do nicely—will come out in front at the top on both sides to serve as the drawstrings. You will need a button of some kind on the flap. A Boy Scout can show you how they tie a turk's head for a neckerchief slide. You can do this in rawhide and then run it up tight into about a ¾" button. Or you can whittle something out of wood and bore two holes through it to run the rawhide through. The two ends of rawhide then run to either side of the button, out through the flap and in again, being cemented on the inside wherever they come through. Figure 21b shows how they run on the inside of the flap. On the outside you just see two stitches of rawhide, symmetrically spaced, one on either side of the button (see fig. 21e).

The inside of the front must be stiffened, but this can be much lighter leather. Regular shoe leather is plenty heavy enough. Figure 21c shows the size and shape. The two holes at the top are the last holes for the draw-strings, and the four at the bottom are for a rawhide loop to go over the button on the cover flap (see fig. 19d & e). These last two illustrations show the sporran partly and fully closed.

The front and back must be connected with a gusset. This should be 2½" wide and of a length to go around the edge of the front and back. If you are having a shoemaker do your sewing, you should carefully cement a strip 1/8" wide on each edge of the gusset and around the front and back. After you assemble them carefully, you can cut off the end of the gusset if you have done it the easy way and started with a gusset that you know is a bit too long. You must cement and assemble it inside out, as you want the seams on the inside when you are done.

It remains only to punch the holes for the drawstrings. Fold the sides in evenly with three inward folds on each side, the center one in the middle of the gusset! The drawstring holes on the front reinforcement must be directly over those in the back. Then the rest of the holes can be accurately lined up. They will not necessarily be the same distance from each other all along; they may fall in pairs, by a little. It's not a bad idea to have the shoemaker put shoelace eyelets in the drawstring holes. Just be sure they are big enough for your rawhide lace! It does no great harm if they are a bit oversize.

PLAIDS

The big job in making an evening plaid is the fringing, and this same style of fringing is found on a piper's plaid and sometimes on the *breacan feile*. There is a problem in the planning and then hours of sitting there twiddling the yarns. The planning problem comes in dividing the sett into units for fringing, but this involves counting threads, which is a little easier when the cross-threads have been pulled out. Any cut edge of a tartan will ravel out readily for a few threads. If you are working on a selvedge, as you will be on an evening plaid, cut the narrowest strip you can off the selvedge, and it will ravel, too. After a while, though, the threads will bunch up and stop being easy to ravel. This happens much sooner with saxony than it does with worsted. All the processes of fringing are much easier with worsted.

When the fringe will no longer run the full length of the tartan, you are going to have to cut it into sections. You will cut perpendicular to the edge, along the boundary between two colors. This makes it much easier to cut as deep as you must without cutting across any threads. Any thread you cut will be lost out of the fringe, and you are going to cut a few. Going down the edge of a color line will minimize this. The cuts should be at least 6" deep and should preferably stop at a boundary between two colors. This makes it easier to get them all to the same depth. In saxony you should have a cut about every six inches. In worsted they need not be as frequent. Next you are going to pull out all the cross threads to the bottom of the cut, leaving you at least six inches of fringe. Twisting the fringe, as we will describe next, shortens it considerably, and it should end up at least 4½" long.

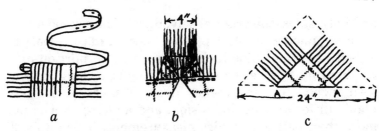

Figure 22. Evening plaid. a) Waist. b) Base for fringe knot. c) Material for fringe knot.

Planning how to divide the fringe comes next. Each tail of the twisted fringe should have 24 to 36 threads in it and should not have more than two colors. If you have —as you do in many setts—a light-colored stripe of eight threads with four black on each side, it is probably better to make a skinny tail of 16 threads, rather than to have three colors in the tail. Plan how many tails you are going to divide the whole sett into before starting! Each tail is now divided in half, and the halves may have mixed colors. For example if you have eight threads of green and sixteen threads of red in a tail, you can divide them twelve and twelve, with eight green and four red in one half. The threads in each half tail are now twisted together in one direction and the half tails laid round each other in the other. If you twist the threads clockwise, you should lay the twisted tails together counterclockwise. When you have the tail laid together all the way out to the end, the very end should be wet with a fabric cement such as Slomon's Sobo Glue, which you should be able to get at any big fabric store. This keeps the end from unravelling. A little practice should make you quite adept at this.

A piper's plaid is simply a piece of double width tartan about 3½ yards long, fringed in this way at both ends. Saxony is cheaper and perfectly satisfactory for the finished job, as there are no pleats to keep pressed. But worsted is far easier to fringe, and if you choose Saxony, you may end up wishing you had not economized.

The evening plaid is a bit more complicated. Start with two yards of double width material, and fringe one end and both sides (the original selvedges). The second end is pleated, much as a kilt is pleated, sewing in the pleats to a depth of about nine inches. This pleated portion may be about nine inches square, or it may be as long as fourteen inches by nine inches deep. Makers of evening plaids differ on this dimension, and as long as it is not more than half your waist measurement, it will do well enough. This end is now fastened to a light strap or heavy tape that will buckle around your waist (see fig 22a).

You now need the knot of fringe that will be fastened by the brooch in front of the shoulder strap. To prepare the place to attach it, the fringed end of the plaid is folded and sewed at the center as shown in figure 22b. The heavy, dotted line shows where the seams should be. The rest of the knot requires a half square of tartan, 24" on the diagonal, cut and fringed as shown in figure 22c. The unfringed diagonal (A-A) is pleated until it measures 4" and is then attached under the tab that is dimensioned 4" in figure 22b.

If you wear the *breacan feile* and have the patience, you can have a truly gaudy one—though of questionable historical accuracy—by fringing the whole top of it—all that comes above the belt. If you do this, you will want a knot of fringe for the brooch, as described above for the evening plaid.

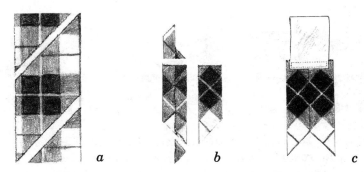

Figure 23. Tartan tabs. a) Strip of selvage, showing cuts. b) Tab folded, trimmed, and turned over. c) Pair of tabs sewed to garter loop.

GARTERS

The commonest garter these days is an elastic with velcro fastening. Figure 23 shows how to make tartan tabs from a strip of selvage, which can be the top that has been cut off of a kilt length. To make a matching pair, cut each tab one full repeat of the tartan, and turn one of them over before folding it.

I am indebted to James D. Scarlett of Milton of Moy in Inverness-shire for a description of the old garter knot— or at least one of the old garter knots. The old portraits

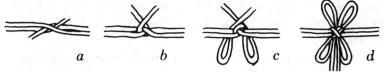

Figure 24. The garter knot. a) Clove hitch. b) Ends crossed upwards. c) First loops tucked in downward. d) Second loops tucked in upward.

do not seem to indicate any perfect uniformity. Start with a clove hitch (fig. 24a). Cross the ends over each other upwards and tuck each in a loop under the knot (fig. 24b & c.) Cross the ends over each other downwards, and tuck crossing loops up under the knot (fig. 24d). Keep on alternating upward and downward loops until the knot is too bulky to continue or until you run out of garter. This knot is, of course, used only with castellated hose, where nothing is turned down over it. I have seen it made with wool hair ties, which didn't look bad at all.

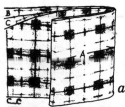
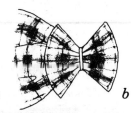
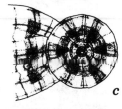

*Figure 25. a) The doubled end of the sash folded back.
b) The rosette pleated and fastened with a rubber band.
c) The corners brought together to complete the rosette.*

THE SASH ROSETTE

To make a rosette of the lady's evening sash, it must be folded double, and the folded end turned back on itself as in figure a. The ends B and C may be equal, but if not, the longer end must be B, the end on the bottom as the rosette is made. The longer the turn-back (A), the larger the rosette, but if A is more than two-thirds of the width of the sash, the rosette cannot be made to lie flat. Midway of the turn-back must be one of the turning points of the sett of the tartan. That is, a mirror set across the sash at the midpoint of the turn-back should see the same thing both ways. If you have a non-reversing tartan, like Buchanan, the midpoint of the turn-back should come between two of the lightest stripes (yellow in the Buchanan).

Now the turned back portion must be gathered into pleats, and a heavy rubber band put around to hold it (see fig. b). This may take two people, one to hold the pleats, and the other to slip the band over all of it. The pleats must be adjusted under the rubber band so that it is exactly at the midpoint of the turned back portion, right on the turning point of the sett of the tartan.

Finally the corners of the turned back portion are brought together to complete the rosette. They may be pinned, or if the rosette is to be permanent, they may be sewed. A decorative Celtic pin hides the rubber band, though another pin must be used from the underside to attach the rosette to the lady's dress. It is pinned to the shoulder much as the sash shown in figure 4b.